THE ULTIMATE
ARSENAL FC
TRIVIA BOOK

A Collection of Amazing Trivia Quizzes
and Fun Facts for Die-Hard Gunners Fans!

Ray Walker

Exclusive Free Book

Crazy Sports Stories

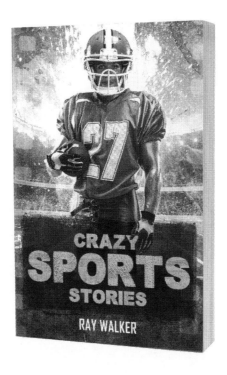

As a thank you for getting a copy of this book I would like to offer you a free copy of my book Crazy Sports Stories which comes packed with interesting stories from your favorite sports such as Football, Hockey, Baseball, Basketball and more.

Grab your free copy over at
RayWalkerMedia.com/Bonus

CONTENTS

INTRODUCTION

Supporters of Arsenal FC, known as "Gooners," are among the proudest and most loyal in the world of soccer. It's easy to see why, since the club is one of the most successful in the UK and inspires a fervent following across the globe.

From the days of the old First and Second Divisions to the Premier League, "the Gunners" have been one of the most consistent and successful soccer clubs on the planet since forming way back in 1886. They've provided fans with plenty of unforgettable moments over the years to help alleviate the pain of the rare low moments.

Whether named Dial Square, Royal Arsenal, Woolwich Arsenal, or simply Arsenal FC, the club's colorful history belongs equally to the great assortment of players, managers, and fans who have made their presence felt at iconic grounds such as "Highbury" and the Emirates Stadium.

This book is a written celebration of the team's peaks and valleys since its inception, as it helps relive and revisit its rich history. You'll have a chance to meet many of the most famous Arsenal characters and learn how each of them contributed to the club's story in their own unique way.

We have looked back at Arsenal's history in quiz form with 12 different chapters, each of them representing a challenging topic. Each section is broken down into 20 challenging quiz questions along with 10 "Did You Know" facts. The chapters' questions are in multiple-choice and true-or-false style formats and the answers are given on a separate page.

This is an ideal way to test yourself on the history of the club and, of course, to challenge other Gooners and football fans to quiz contests. The book will help refresh your knowledge of your favorite team and help you prepare for any challenges that come your way.

Also, you can use the book to teach other fans about the significance of Arsenal legends such as Cliff Bastin, Ian Wright, David Seaman, Thierry Henry, Tony Adams, Patrick Vieira, David O'Leary, etc. The top managers are also included, such as Herbert Chapman, George Graham, and the incomparable Arsène Wenger.

The information and statistics used are current up to January 1st, 2021, but Arsenal's legacy will surely carry on for many years to come.

CHAPTER 1:

ORIGINS & HISTORY

QUIZ TIME!

1. In which year was the club founded?

    a. 1883

    b. 1884

    c. 1885

    d. 1886

2. The club was originally known as Dial Square FC.

    a. True

    b. False

3. What official league did Arsenal join in 1893?

    a. Football League

    b. London Football Association

    c. The Combination

    d. Football Alliance

4. Arsenal played its very first match against which club?

    a. Queens Park Rangers

    b. Milwall FC

c. Eastern Wanderers

d. Southampton FC

5. As of 2020, how many times have Arsenal been relegated?

    a. Never

    b. Three times

    c. Once

    d. Twice

6. Which man was not one of the original three founders of Arsenal FC?

    a. John Humble

    b. Elijah Watkins

    c. David Danskin

    d. Bill Shankly

7. Woolwich Arsenal was the first team from Southern London to join the Football League.

    a. True

    b. False

8. Where did the club play its first-ever match?

    a. Plumstead Common

    b. Isle of Dogs

    c. Manor Ground

    d. Invicta Ground

9. Who bought the club in 1904, preventing it from voluntary liquidation?

    a. Herbert Chapman

    b. Henry Norris

    c. George Allison

    d. Tom Whittaker

10. Which year did the team move to Arsenal Stadium, commonly known as Highbury Stadium?

    a. 1904

    b. 1920

    c. 1910

    d. 1913

11. How many games did the squad win in its first season in the Second Division?

    a. 14

    b. 8

    c. 12

    d. 16

12. The club competed for the FA Cup in its second season.

    a. True

    b. False

13. When the team was relegated in 1912-13, how many league matches did it lose that season?

    a. 23

    b. 20

    c. 27

    d. 30

14. What is the club's nickname?

    a. The Gunners

    b. The Clockmen

c. Highbury Boys

d. The Reds

15. The club was a founding member of which short-lived league?

 a. Combination League

 b. London League Premier Division

 c. Southern District Combination

 d. United League

16. The Arsenal motto is Latin for "Our weapons are raised for the King."

 a. True

 b. False

17. In 1901, the club introduced a crest that featured how many cannons?

 a. 1

 b. 2

 c. 3

 d. 4

18. How many points did the squad record in its first season in the First Division?

 a. 33

 b. 67

 c. 44

 d. 38

19. Which club did Arsenal face in its first Premier League game in 1992?

a. Liverpool

b. Oldham Athletic

c. Blackburn Rovers

d. Norwich City

20. The team was promoted to the First Division in 1904-05.

a. True

b. False

QUIZ ANSWERS

1. D – 1886

2. A – True

3. A – Football League

4. C – Eastern Wanderers

5. C – Once

6. D – Bill Shankly

7. A – True

8. B – Isle of Dogs

9. B – Henry Norris

10. D – 1913

11. C – 12

12. B – False

13. A – 23

14. A – The Gunners

15. D – United League

16. B – False

17. C – 3

18. A – 33

19. D – Norwich City

20. A – True

DID YOU KNOW?

1. The Arsenal Football Club of the English Premier League was founded in October 1886 when employees of the Royal Arsenal munitions factory in the Woolwich area of London named their team Dial Square. The club changed its name to Royal Arsenal just a month later and, in 1893, the name was changed again to Woolwich Arsenal. Twenty years later, the club became The Arsenal and soon after became known simply as Arsenal.

2. The club's nickname is "the Gunners' and Arsenal supporters are known as "Gooners." The club's motto is the Latin saying "victoria concordia crescit," which means "victory through harmony" in English. Arsenal and Emirates Stadium are currently owned by Kroenke Sports & Entertainment, an American company based in Denver, Colorado, that is owned by Stan and Josh Kroenke.

3. In 1893, Royal Arsenal became the first southern English and London club to join the Football League when the team started out in the Second Division. It was promoted to the First Division in 1904 and, as of 2020, has been relegated just once, in 1913. Arsenal owns the longest continuous streak in England's top professional football division.

4. The team's first home ground was at Plumstead Common; they also played games at the Manor Ground and Invicta

Ground. However, in 1913, they moved to Arsenal Stadium in the Highbury area of North London and the ground soon became known by fans simply as "Highbury." In 2006, the club built a new ground, which was and is still named Emirates Stadium. It is the fourth-largest soccer ground in England with a capacity of 60,704.

5. The first London football club to turn professional was Royal Arsenal back in 1891. The first pieces of silverware added to their trophy cabinet were the London Charity Cup and the Kent Senior Cup in the 1889-90 season and the London Senior Cup the following campaign. The Royal Arsenal reserves also managed to beat the first team to a trophy by hoisting the Kent Junior Cup in 1890.

6. Royal Arsenal came close to going bankrupt in 1910 when their home attendances fell due to financial problems among munitions workers, as well as the arrival of other soccer clubs in London. However, businessmen William Hall and Henry Norris got involved with the team and, by 1913, they had moved it to Highbury. Arsenal was promoted back to the First Division in 1919 by a vote when the division was expanded following World War I.

7. Arsenal won the English FA Cup for the first time in 1930 under manager Herbert Chapman. He then led the squad to its first league championship in 1930-31 and followed up with another First Division title the following season.

8. For most of the club's history, the team's home uniform colors have featured red shirts with white sleeves along

with white shorts. The club's shirts have been various shades of red over the years and its home red socks once featured blue and white hoops. The white sleeves were added to the shirt in 1933 when the red became a brighter shade. In 1966-67, the team experimented with all-red shirts for just one season.

9. Arsenal's away colors were often navy blue or white with a kit featuring yellow shirts and blue shorts being introduced in 1969. A navy blue and green away kit was worn in 1982–83 for one season and the club then reverted to yellow and blue. However, in 1994, the team's away colors were changed again to two-tone blue shirts and shorts and they have been changed several times since, with third kits also being introduced.

10. There is also an Arsenal women's team, which, as of January 2021, had won 58 trophies to be recognized as the most successful side in English women's soccer. They won all three major English trophies in 2008-09: the FA Women's Premier League, the FA Women's Premier League Cup, and the FA Women's Cup. The squad has also won the UEFA Women's Cup and UEFA Women's Champions League. The team, now known as Arsenal Women FC, was founded in 1987 and plays in the Women's Super League. Home games are played at Meadow Park in Boreham Wood.

CHAPTER 2:

THE CAPTAIN CLASS

QUIZ TIME!

1. Who was the club's first captain?

    a. Arthur Brown
    b. David Danskin
    c. Morris Bates
    d. Bill Julian

2. In the 1891-92 season, six different players served as captain.

    a. True
    b. False

3. Which player was named captain in 2019, replacing Granit Xhaka?

    a. Pierre-Emerick Aubameyang
    b. Laurent Koscielny
    c. Willian
    d. Mesut Özil

4. Who was Arsenal's first captain to be born outside of the British Isles?

   a. William Gallas

   b. Cesc Fàbregas

   c. Patrick Vieira

   d. Thierry Henry

5. Which player was stripped of the captaincy in 2008 after criticizing teammates in the media?

   a. Eduardo

   b. Abou Diaby

   c. William Gallas

   d. Thierry Henry

6. Which player captained the club during the 2011-12 season?

   a. Carl Jenkinson

   b. Francis Coquelin

   c. Theo Walcott

   d. Robin van Persie

7. Alan Smith was the first captain of Arsenal in the Premier League era.

   a. True

   b. False

8. Who was the club's captain in 1986-87?

   a. Kenny Sansom

   b. David O'Leary

   c. Graham Rix

   d. Pat Rice

9. Which player was the club's youngest permanent captain, given the position at the age of 20?

    a. Tony Adams
    b. Cesc Fàbregas
    c. Eddie Kelly
    d. Terry Neill

10. Who is the longest-serving captain in Arsenal's history as of 2020?

    a. Eddie Hapgood
    b. Percy Sands
    c. Frank McLintock
    d. Tony Adams

11. How many players captained served as full-time captains between 2010 and 2020?

    a. 6
    b. 7
    c. 8
    d. 9

12. Pierre-Emerick Aubameyang was the club's first captain born outside of Europe.

    a. True
    b. False

13. Which player was captain from 1963 to 1966?

    a. George Eastham
    b. Don Howe
    c. Vic Groves
    d. Bob McNab

14. Who led the club to its first-ever trophy in 1890?

    a. Billy Blyth
    b. Frank Bradshaw
    c. Morris Bates
    d. Sandy Robertson

15. How many goalkeepers have been named full-time captain as of 2020?

    a. 3
    b. 8
    c. 12
    d. 0

16. Alan Ball captained the club for only one season, 1974-75.

    a. True
    b. False

17. The majority of the club's captains have hailed from which nation?

    a. England
    b. Scotland
    c. Ireland
    d. Wales

18. How many seasons was Tony Adams the captain of Arsenal?

    a. 10
    b. 13
    c. 14
    d. 17

19. Which of these players did not serve as a club captain between 1955 and 1957?

   a. Don Roper
   b. Cliff Holton
   c. Peter Goring
   d. Vic Groves

20. Arsenal has had fewer than 40 captains as of 2020.

   a. True
   b. False

QUIZ ANSWERS

1. B – David Danskin

2. A – True

3. A – Pierre-Emerick Aubameyang

4. C – Patrick Vieira

5. C – William Gallas

6. D – Robin van Persie

7. B – False

8. A – Kenny Sansom

9. D – Terry Neill

10. D – Tony Adams

11. C – 8

12. A – False

13. A – George Eastham

14. C – Morris Bates

15. D – 0

16. B – False

17. A – England

18. C – 14

19. D – Vic Groves

20. B – False

DID YOU KNOW?

1. Arsenal has had over 60 full-time captains since the club started out as Dial Square FC in 1886. The current skipper as of January 2021 is forward Pierre-Emerick Aubameyang, who took over from Granit Xhaka in 2019. The club had six captains in the 1890-91 and 1891-92 seasons as they shared the duties on a rotating month-to-month basis. In addition, Eddie Kelly was listed as team captain in 1975-76 with Terry Mancini being the club captain.

2. The club's first captain, in 1886, was David Danskin of Scotland. The mechanical engineer was one of the founding members of Dial Square FC. He helped form the club after moving to London in 1885 and taking a job at the Dial Square workshop, which was located at the Royal Arsenal. He skippered the side in its very first outing on Dec. 11, 1886, against Eastern Wanderers, which resulted in a 6-0 victory. However, he suffered an injury in January 1889 and soon retired, with Arthur Brown then taking over the captaincy.

3. Between 1886 and 1980, all Arsenal captains were from the British Isles, either England, Scotland, Wales, the Republic of Ireland, or Northern Ireland. The first foreign-born skipper was French international midfielder Patrick Vieira, who was born in Senegal. He captained the squad from 2002 to 2005. Since Vieira, all 10 full-time Arsenal skippers have been born outside of the British Isles.

4. Former English international defender Tony Adams was the longest-serving captain at Arsenal, wearing the armband from 1988 to 2002. Midfielder Percy Sands of England is listed as being the skipper from 1906 to 1919, but this includes several unofficial seasons during World War I. Sands played 350 games during his 17 years of service with the club.

5. Since the English Premier League was formed in 1992, the Gunners have had a dozen different full-time captains: Tony Adams, Patrick Vieira, Thierry Henry, William Gallas, Cesc Fàbregas, Robin van Persie, Thomas Vermaelen, Mikel Arteta, Per Mertesacker, Laurent Koscielny, Granit Xhaka, and Pierre-Emerick Aubameyang.

6. The club's first long-term captain was Jimmy Jackson of Scotland, the defender/midfielder who skippered the side from 1901 to 1905. Jackson played in Australia, where he was raised, and returned to Scotland in 1893. He then headed to England and played with Newcastle United in 1897 before joining Woolwich Arsenal in 1899. Jackson spent six seasons with Arsenal and was the club's first captain in the First Division in 1904. Jackson played just over 200 league and cup games for the Gunners. His son, James Jackson, later played for Liverpool, while son Archie played with Sunderland and Tranmere Rovers.

7. English defender Eddie Hapgood had the good fortune of wearing the armband for club and country. He signed for Arsenal in 1927 and took over from Alex James as captain

in 1937. He led the team to the league title in 1937–38 and finished his career with a pair of FA Cup medals and five league championships. Hapgood captained Arsenal until the mid-1940s and played 30 times for England, wearing the armband for 21 of those contests. He played over 400 times for Arsenal and also made money as a fashion model.

8. The club's skipper from 1947 to 1954 was English left-half Joe Mercer. He played with Everton from 1932 to 1946 and then appeared with Arsenal from 1946 to 1955. He won the First Division and the Charity Shield twice. He led the Gunners to the FA Cup in 1950 and was also named the FWA Footballer of the Year that season. Mercer broke his leg in 1954 and retired after 275 matches with Arsenal. He played five times for England, managed several clubs after retiring, and was caretaker manager for England for seven games in 1974.

9. Belgian international defender Thomas Vermaelen joined the Gunners in 2009 and captained the side from 2012 until joining Barcelona in 2014 for a reported £15 million. He was bought by Arsenal from Dutch side Ajax initially for a reported €10 million and scored in his Gunners' debut. Vermaelen was soon nicknamed "the Verminator" and helped the London side to the FA Cup in 2013-14 and was named to the 2009-10 PFA Premier League Team of the Year.

10. Mikel Arteta, who is Arsenal's manager as of January 2021, served as the club's captain between 2014 and 2016.

The Spanish international midfielder played with Barcelona, Paris Saint-Germain, Glasgow Rangers, Real Sociedad, and Everton before joining the Gunners in August 2011. The playmaker added 16 goals in 150 appearances with Arsenal before retiring in 2016. He won two straight Charity Shield trophies and FA Cups with the club in 2014 and 2015.

CHAPTER 3:

AMAZING MANAGERS

QUIZ TIME!

1. Who acted as the club's first team trainer from 1894 to 1897?

    a. Arthur Brown
    b. Sam Hollis
    c. David Danskin
    d. Thomas Brown Mitchell

2. Before 1894, Arsenal was managed by a collective group of directors.

    a. True
    b. False

3. How many matches did Arsène Wenger manage?

    a. 977
    b. 1,235
    c. 1,193
    d. 1,236

4. Which manager lost 122 of 309 matches while he was in charge of the side?

    a. Tom Whittaker
    b. Leslie Knighton
    c. Terry Neill
    d. George Morrell

5. This manager was in charge of the club from June 1995 to August 1996.

    a. George Graham
    b. Stewart Houston
    c. Bruce Rioch
    d. Pat Rice

6. This manager's winning percentage stood at 50.21.

    a. Phil Kelso
    b. George Allison
    c. Harry Bradshaw
    d. William Elcoat

7. Arsène Wenger had a career winning percentage of 57.25 percent.

    a. True
    b. False

8. How many people managed Arsenal in the year 2019?

    a. 1
    b. 3
    c. 2
    d. 4

9. How many goals did Arsenal score while under George Graham's management?

    a. 534
    b. 601
    c. 672
    d. 711

10. Who was named the club's manager on June 20, 1966?

    a. Bertie Mee
    b. Steve Burtenshaw
    c. Billy Wright
    d. George Swindin

11. How many temporary caretaker-managers has Arsenal appointed as of 2020?

    a. 6
    b. 7
    c. 8
    d. 9

12. Terry Neill was appointed as Arsenal's manager only two years after he retired.

    a. True
    b. False

13. Who succeeded Arsène Wenger as manager on May 23, 2019?

    a. Glenn Roeder
    b. Unai Emery
    c. Freddie Ljungberg
    d. Mikel Arteta

14. Before becoming Arsenal's full-time boss in 2019, Mikel Arteta was an assistant to this legendary manager.

    a. Jurgen Klopp
    b. Antonio Conte
    c. José Mourinho
    d. Pep Guardiola

15. How many League Cups did Arsène Wenger win with Arsenal?

    a. 3
    b. 5
    c. 7
    d. 0

16. Phil Kelso has a win percentage of 36.57, the lowest of any Arsenal manager with a minimum of 100 games.

    a. True
    b. False

17. Leslie Knighton won how many games as manager between May 1919 and May 1925?

    a. 42
    b. 84
    c. 105
    d. 121

18. This future manager commentated on the first radio broadcast of an FA Cup final in 1927.

    a. James McEwen
    b. Herbert Chapman

c. Joe Shaw

d. George Allison

19. Which manager led the club to its first FA Cup championship?

   a. Herbert Chapman

   b. Joe Shaw

   c. George Allison

   d. Leslie Knighton

20. As of 2020, three caretakers have been promoted to full-time managers of Arsenal.

   a. True

   b. False

QUIZ ANSWERS

1. B – Sam Hollis

2. A – True

3. B – 1,235

4. D – George Morrell

5. C – Bruce Rioch

6. C – Harry Bradshaw

7. A – True

8. C – 2

9. D – 711

10. A – Bertie Mee

11. C – 8

12. B – False

13. B – Unai Emery

14. D – Pep Guardiola

15. D – 0

16. B – False

17. C – 105

18. D – George Allison

19. A – Herbert Chapman

20. A – True

DID YOU KNOW?

1. After being formed as Dial Square in 1886, the club spent its first several seasons playing friendly games and participating in various cup tournaments with no official manager being named. Between 1893 and 1897, it's widely believed the management of the team was looked after by a committee of directors with the first permanent manager being named in 1897. The first to hold the job was Thomas Mitchell of Scotland, who remained in the position until resigning in March 1898.

2. Some sources list Sam Hollis as the club's first official manager but it's argued that the job he held with the team between 1894 and 1897 was simply as team trainer. The native of Nottingham, England, then left the club in April 1987 to become the manager of Bristol City. With Hollis included as a manager, Arsenal has had a total of 20 full-time bosses and eight caretaker-managers.

3. Those who have managed the club since 1894 are Sam Hollis, Thomas Mitchell, William Elcoat, Arthur Kennedy, Harry Bradshaw, Phil Kelso, George Morrell, James McEwen, Leslie Knighton, Herbert Chapman, Joe Shaw, George Allison, Tom Whittaker, Jack Crayston, George Swindin, Billy Wright, Bertie Mee, Terry Neill, Don Howe, Steve Burtenshaw, George Graham, Stewart Houston, Bruce Rioch, Pat Rice, Arsène Wenger, Unai Emery,

Freddie Ljungberg, and the current manager as of January 2021, Mikel Arteta.

4. When it comes to winning silverware, the most successful manager in club history has been Arsène Wenger. His haul consists of three Premier League titles, a record seven FA Cups, and seven Community Shields. In addition, Wenger is the Gunners' longest-serving manager. He held the post from October 1, 1996, to May 13, 2018. He was in charge for 1,235 matches with a record of 707 wins, 280 draws, and 248 losses for a winning percentage of 57.25.

5. Arsène Wenger was known for his feud with Manchester United boss Sir Alex Ferguson, who called Wenger a novice when he arrived at Arsenal from managing in Japan. Ferguson always claimed his team was better even after Wenger's squad went unbeaten in 2003-04. Sir Alex liked belittling Wenger in the press and the two managers refused to shake each other's hand after games several times. The rivalry hit a high point in 2004 when Ferguson's side halted Arsenal's 49-match unbeaten streak at Old Trafford. Somebody threw a slice of pizza at the Man United boss in the tunnel after the contest, leading to a brawl between the players.

6. José Mourinho also enjoyed needling Arsène Wenger while the two were managing in the Premier League. Mourinho called Wenger a specialist in failure while the Arsenal boss criticized Mourinho's defensive style of play by saying he parked the bus. Mourinho also said Arsenal

won just 50 percent of its league games with Wenger in charge while Wenger called his counterpart disrespectful and stupid. Even after Mourinho departed the Premier League for Real Madrid, he continued the feud by labeling Wenger Monsieur Polite. The managers went at it in the press for years with one of the most famous insults coming in 2005 when Mourinho called Wenger a voyeur.

7. The first manager to win silverware with Arsenal was Herbert Chapman, who managed the side from June 11, 1925, to his death on January 6, 1934. Chapman led the side to the First Division crown in 1930-31 and again in 1932-33. He also captured the FA Cup in 1930 and the Charity Shield in 1930, 1931, and 1933. Known as one of the sport's great innovators, Chapman passed away from pneumonia at the age of 55. He was in charge of the team for 411 games with a mark of 204 wins, 97 draws, and 110 losses for a winning percentage of 49.64.

8. Pat Rice and Joe Shaw hold the best winning percentages for the club, but Rice managed just four games in September 1996 while Shaw was in charge for 23 contests between Jan. 6 and May 28, 1934. Rice, a former Gunners' defender who played over 500 times for the team, won three and lost one of the four games under his charge. Shaw was also a former club defender as well as team captain and played over 300 games with the squad. Shaw took over as caretaker after Herbert Chapman passed away and posted a record of 14 wins, three draws, and six losses to help the Gunners win the First Division title in 1933-34.

9. Another popular and successful Arsenal manager was George Graham, who helped the club haul in an FA Cup, two First Division titles, two League Cups, a Charity Shield, and a UEFA Cup Winner's Cup between May 14, 1986, and Feb. 21, 1995. The Scotsman played over 200 games for the Gunners between 1966 and 1972 and won 225 of his 460 games as manager with 133 draws and 102 defeats for a 48.91 winning percentage. His 1992-93 squad became the first to win the League Cup and FA Cup double in England. However, he was fired for accepting an illegal payment of £425,000 from a Norwegian player agent after signing two of his clients. Graham was also banned by the Football Association for a year for the scandal.

10. Arsenal didn't have to look far for their first 24 managers; they all hailed from Scotland, England, or Northern Ireland. However, the last four have come from the European mainland. Arsène Wenger of France was the first foreign-born manager, followed in succession by Unai Emery of Spain, Freddie Ljungberg of Sweden, and Mikel Arteta of Spain, who still held the job as of January 2021.

CHAPTER 4:

GOALTENDING GREATS

QUIZ TIME!

1. Which keeper made 564 appearances for Arsenal?

    a. Pat Jennings
    b. David Seaman
    c. Bob Wilson
    d. Jens Lehmann

2. In 2018-19, David Ospina replaced Petr Čech as the club's primary keeper.

    a. True
    b. False

3. As of January 2021, how many keepers had made at least 100 appearances for the club?

    a. 9
    b. 12
    c. 15
    d. 18

4. Which keeper made his one and only Premier League appearance for the club on the final day of the 2006-07 season?

   a. Vito Mannone
   b. Rami Shaaban
   c. Mart Poom
   d. Alan Miller

5. How many league matches did Petr Čech play in total for Arsenal?

   a. 88
   b. 96
   c. 108
   d. 110

6. Which keeper played 1,498 league minutes in 2014-15?

   a. Matt Macey
   b. Wojciech Szczęsny
   c. David Ospina
   d. Emiliano Martinez

7. After retiring in 2019, Arsenal keeper Petr Čech signed with a semi-professional ice hockey team, Guildford Phoenix.

   a. True
   b. False

8. How many clean sheets did David Seaman record in league matches in 1993-941?

   a. 12
   b. 13

c. 18

d. 20

9. Which keeper won four Premier League Golden Glove Awards?

   a. David Seaman

   b. Wojciech Szczęsny

   c. David Ospina

   d. Petr Čech

10. How many league matches did Bernd Leno draw during the 2019-20 season?

    a. 7

    b. 13

    c. 15

    d. 17

11. Which keeper did not make an appearance for Arsenal in any match in 2008-09?

    a. Vito Mannone

    b. Łukasz Fabiański

    c. Jens Lehmann

    d. Manuel Almunia

12. In 2003-04, Jens Lehmann did not lose a single Premier League match.

    a. True

    b. False

13. Which keeper made over 300 appearances between 1963 and 1974?

a. Bob Wilson

b. Jack Kelsey

c. Jim Furnell

d. Jimmy Rimmer

14. Who was the club's first goalkeeper to appear in more than 100 matches?

a. Ernest Williamson

b. Jock Robson

c. Dan Lewis

d. Jimmy Ashcroft

15. How many league matches did David Ospina win in 2014-15?

a. 9

b. 11

c. 13

d. 16

16. Stuart Taylor made 54 saves in 10 domestic league matches in 2001-02.

a. True

b. False

17. Emiliano Martinez won a total of how many games in all competitions in 2019-20?

a. 22

b. 21

c. 19

d. 15

18. Who recorded 10 clean sheets in 29 domestic league games in 2009-10?

    a. Wojciech Szczęsny
    b. Łukasz Fabiański
    c. Manuel Almunia
    d. Jens Lehmann

19. Of the seven penalty kicks Bernd Leno faced in 2018-19 league matches, how many did he allow in?

    a. 7
    b. 6
    c. 5
    d. 4

20. In his first season with Arsenal, Alex Manninger recorded six consecutive clean sheets in domestic league matches.

    a. True
    b. False

QUIZ ANSWERS

1. B – David Seaman

2. B – False

3. D – 18

4. C – Mart Poom

5. D – 110

6. B – Wojciech Szczęsny

7. A – True

8. C – 20

9. D – Petr Čech

10. B – 13

11. C – Jens Lehmann

12. A – True

13. A – Bob Wilson

14. D – Jimmy Ashcroft

15. C – 13

16. B – False

17. D – 15

18. C – Manuel Almunia

19. A – 7

20. A – True

DID YOU KNOW?

1. Legendary Gunners' keeper David Seaman debuted with Leeds United in 1981, followed by stints at Peterborough United, Birmingham City, and Queens Park Rangers before joining Arsenal in 1990. He played with the club until 2003 and then spent his final campaign with Manchester City. With Arsenal, the pony-tailed goalie won three league titles, four FA Cups, a League Cup, and a European Cup Winners Cup by regularly making spectacular saves. Seaman made over 560 appearances with the club to set a record for goalkeepers and e also made 75 appearances for England.

2. Former Czech Republic international Petr Čech made a name for himself in the Premier League with Chelsea between 2004 and 2015 by winning several trophies and awards. He made his way to the Emirates Stadium in June 2015 for a fee of approximately £10 million when he signed a four-year deal amid death threats from some Chelsea supporters. He appeared in 139 matches with the Gunners until 2019, when he retired and dabbled in ice hockey. He then surprised many by rejoining Chelsea for the 2020-21 campaign as an emergency keeper. Čech helped Arsenal win two Community Shields and an FA Cup and holds numerous international and Premier League records for a goalkeeper including a league-leading 202 clean sheets.

3. Former German international Jens Lehmann joined Arsenal in July 2003 from Borussia Dortmund to replace

David Seaman. He had an incredible first season with the club, as the squad went unbeaten for the entire Premier League campaign with Lehmann playing every game. He wasn't perfect during his Gunners career but helped his side win a league title, an FA Cup, and a Community Shield. He left in 2008 only to return in March 2011, when Arsenal was short of goalkeepers due to injuries. The 41-year-old played a month later when scheduled starter Manuel Almunia was injured in a warmup. Lehmann won the game 3-1 in what was his 200th and final appearance for the team. He was the oldest Arsenal player to appear in a Premier League match.

4. Former England international Frank Moss tended goal for Arsenal between 1931 and 1937 but may be more famous for scoring a crucial goal for the side. While battling for the First Division title in March 1935, the Gunners needed to beat Everton away at Goodison Park. However, Moss dislocated a shoulder during the match and was replaced in goal. But with no substitutes in those days, he moved to left wing and scored the insurance marker in a 2-0 victory to help win the crown. Moss is the only Arsenal keeper as of 2020 to score an official top-flight competitive goal and he helped the team win three straight league titles.

5. Regarded by many as one of Northern Ireland's greatest goalkeepers ever, Pat Jennings joined Arsenal in August 1977 from Tottenham Hotspur after spending 13 years with the North London rivals. Jennings then spent eight years with the Gunners and helped them win the FA Cup

in 1979 while finishing as runners-up in 1978 and 1980 as well as European Cup Winners' Cup runners-up in 1980. Jennings played 327 games with Arsenal before retiring in 1985. In February 1983, he became the first player in English soccer to appear in 1,000 league games.

6. Jack Kelsey played 41 times for Wales and more than 350 times for Arsenal between 1949 and 1963. He was the team's number one for most of the 1950s after taking over from George Swindin and won the league title in 1952-53. Kelsey was regarded as a goalkeeping innovator as he was one of the first to sprint out of the 18-yard-box to confront attackers. It's also believed he rubbed chewing gum on his hands before games to get a better grip on the ball.

7. With over 300 appearances to his name, Bob Wilson is rightfully recognized by many as one of Arsenal's top goalkeepers. The English-born Wilson played just twice for Scotland, but he enjoyed a fine club career after joining the Gunners in 1963 as an amateur from Wolverhampton Wanderers. He played until retiring in 1974 at the age of 32 and then spent 28 years as the Gunners' goalkeeping coach. Wilson is also well known in the UK for his broadcasting and charity work. The Arsenal player of the year for 1970 helped his side win an FA Cup and First Division double in 1970-71 as well as the Inter-Cities Fairs Cup the previous season.

8. George Swindin managed Arsenal between 1958 and 1962 but was also a stellar goalie for the side from 1936 to 1954. He was bought from Bradford City for £4,000 and would go

on to play 297 official games with the club. His career was interrupted by World War II when he became a policeman as well as a physical training teacher with the army. Swindin won three league titles with the Gunners as well as an FA Cup before retiring and turning to management.

9. When Alex Manninger arrived in 1997, it was to take over for the injured David Seaman. The Austrian international then posted a club-record six straight clean sheets, including a 1-0 win over Manchester United at Old Trafford. Manninger was named Premier League Player of the Month that March but then gave way when Seaman returned. He also saved a shootout penalty in the FA Cup quarterfinals as Arsenal won the league and cup double that season. Although Manninger played just seven league games that season and 10 were needed to be awarded a winners' medal, he was still given one due to his contribution to the title run. He played just 64 times before leaving in 2001 but was more than reliable when called upon.

10. John Lukic enjoyed two stints with the Gunners, from 1983 to 1990 as Pat Jennings' replacement and again between 1996 and 2001. He was originally signed from Leeds United and returned to Leeds between his stints with Arsenal. Lukic played a total of 298 games with the Gunners and helped them win the League Cup in 1987, the First Division title in 1988-89, and the Charity Shield in 1999. When he returned to Leeds before rejoining Arsenal, he won the First Division title in 1991-92 and the Charity Shield in 1992.

CHAPTER 5:

DARING DEFENDERS

QUIZ TIME!

1. Which defender played a total of 2,611 minutes in the 2018-19 Premier League season?

   a. Sokratis Papastathopoulos
   b. Nacho Monreal
   c. Shkodran Mustafi
   d. Sead Kolašinac

2. Tony Adams holds the club record for the most appearances by a defender.

   a. True
   b. False

3. How many yellow cards did Ashley Cole accrue during his time with Arsenal?

   a. 18
   b. 29
   c. 21
   d. 33

4. In the 2015-16 Premier League, which defender tallied 5 assists?

   a. Laurent Koscielny
   b. Gabriel Paulista
   c. Nacho Monreal
   d. Héctor Bellerín

5. Which defender scored 6 goals in all competitions in 2011-12?

   a. Thomas Vermaelen
   b. Laurent Koscielny
   c. Bacary Sagna
   d. Per Mertesacker

6. How many appearances did Sol Campbell make in all competitions for Arsenal in 2003-04?

   a. 37
   b. 44
   c. 49
   d. 50

7. Frank McLintock originally played as a striker for Arsenal before being moved to the back line.

   a. True
   b. False

8. Who played a total of 3,029 minutes in the 2012-13 Premier League season?

   a. Barcary Sagna
   b. Per Mertesacker

    c. Ignasi Miguel

    d. Carl Jenkinson

9. Which defender played over 600 games for the club?

    a. Pat Rice

    b. Peter Simpson

    c. Lee Dixon

    d. Martin Keown

10. How many appearances did David O'Leary make for Arsenal in all competitions?

    a. 621

    b. 669

    c. 685

    d. 722

11. Which defender completed 1,481 passes in 2019-20 domestic league games?

    a. Sead Kolašinac

    b. David Luiz

    c. Calum Chambers

    d. Sokratis Papastathopoulos

12. In 2018-19, three different defenders each scored a total of three goals in the Premier League.

    a. True

    b. False

13. Which defender made 501 appearances for Arsenal?

    a. Martin Keown

    b. Peter Simpson

c. Eddie Hapgood

d. Peter Storey

14. Which defender played fewer than 200 games for the Gunners?

    a. Steve Bould

    b. Eddie Hapgood

    c. Nigel Winterburn

    d. Duncan McNichol

15. Which defender received two red cards in all competitions in 2016-17?

    a. Laurent Koscielny

    b. Rob Holding

    c. Calum Chambers

    d. Mathieu Debuchy

16. Five defenders have played over 600 times for Arsenal.

    a. True

    b. False

17. Which defender scored a total of 28 goals with Arsenal?

    a. Nigel Winterburn

    b. Lee Dixon

    c. David O'Leary

    d. Pat Rice

18. How many yellow cards did Giles Grimandi receive in the 1999-2000 Premier League?

    a. 6

    b. 7

c. 8

d. 9

19. Which defender did not make up part of Arsenal's famous "Back Four"?

    a. Lee Dixon

    b. Tony Adams

    c. Martin Keown

    d. Steve Bould

20. Tony Adams scored over 45 career goals for Arsenal.

    a. True

    b. False

QUIZ ANSWERS

1. C – Shkodran Mustafi

2. B – False

3. B – 29

4. D – Héctor Bellerín

5. A – Thomas Vermaelen

6. C – 49

7. B – False

8. B – Per Mertesacker

9. C – Lee Dixon

10. D – 722

11. B – David Luiz

12. B – False

13. D – Peter Storey

14. D –Duncan McNichol

15. A – Laurent Koscielny

16. B – False

17. B – Lee Dixon

18. D – 9

19. C – Martin Keown

20. A – True

DID YOU KNOW?

1. As of January 2021, former central defender David O'Leary still holds the record for most appearances for Arsenal at 722, with 558 of these being league outings. Although he was born in England, O'Leary played with the Republic of Ireland 68 times and served as Gunners' captain for approximately 18 months between 1980 and 1983. He made his big-league debut as a 17-year-old and left the team for Leeds United on a free transfer in 1993. In between, the calm, cool and collected defender chipped in with 14 goals and helped the squad win two league titles, FA Cups, and League Cups as well as a Charity Shield.

2. Tony Adams, who was Arsenal's longest-serving skipper, was also an English international captain who suited up 669 times for the club between 1983 and 2002 and contributed close to 50 goals. Known as "Mr. Arsenal," Adams helped the team capture four league titles, three FA Cups, two League Cups, the Football League Centenary Trophy, the European Cup Winners' Cup, and a couple of Charity Shields. Adams played his entire career with the Gunners and also won numerous personal awards. He's the only player in English football history to have captained a league championship side in three different decades, and now a statue sits outside of Emirates Stadium in his honor.

3. Lee Dixon played for the club from 1988 to 2002 and left with over 600 games under his belt. The defensive mainstay signed from Stoke City and proceeded to collect four league titles with Arsenal along with three FA Cups, three Charity Shields, and a UEFA Cup Winners' Cup. He made the PFA Team of the Year on two occasions and during his career, Dixon managed to play on 91 of England's 92 professional club soccer grounds, the only exception being Fulham's Craven Cottage. Dixon became a well-known broadcasting pundit after hanging up his boots.

4. Pat Rice played for Arsenal, served as captain and assistant manager, and also took over as caretaker manager for a brief time. He appeared in 528 contests between 1967 and 1980. In 1970-71, he helped the club hoist the League and FA Cup double and then added another FA Cup winner's medal in 1979. Rice was regarded for his modesty and hard work and with a little luck could have won a few more winners' medals. While captaining the side, the Gunners made three consecutive FA Cup Finals between 1978 and 80 but won just one of them. They also dropped the European Cup Winners' Cup final in 1980 by penalty shootout.

5. Scottish international Frank McLintock played just over 400 times with Arsenal between 1964 and 1973, tallying 32 goals. He started his Gunners career as a wing/back and often focused on attacking rather than defending. However, he later reverted to central defense and he thrived in his new role. He helped the team win the 1970 European Fairs Cup and the League and FA Cup double

the very next season. McLintock was named the Football Writers' Association's Footballer of the Year for 1971 and was the Gunners' player of the year in 1968.

6. Martin Keown was another long-time Arsenal player who appeared in 449 outings between 1985 and 1986 and from 1993 to 2004. In between, he was sold to Aston Villa in 1986, after spells with Villa and Everton, he returned to the Gunners in February 1993. The English international center-back went on to win three league titles, three FA Cups, three Community Shields, and a European Cup Winners' Cup with Arsenal. The quick and hard-tackling Keown then left on a free transfer to join Leicester City and was another of many players who entered the world of coaching and broadcasting after retiring.

7. Sol Campbell's stay at Arsenal may have been short but it was certainly sweet. He played just over 200 games between 2001 and 2008 and again in 2010. He originally joined from rivals Tottenham Hotspur on a controversial free transfer and helped the club win two league titles and FA Cups as well as making it to the UEFA Champions League final in 2006. The gifted English international center-back was also named to the PFA Team of the Year for 2002-03 and 2003-04. He left Arsenal in July 2006 but returned in January 2010 for the remainder of the campaign before leaving for Newcastle United two months later.

8. Between 1999 and 2006, one of Arsenal's most talented defenders was English international Ashley Cole, who was

also known for his attacking runs. Cole appeared in 228 contests with the squad and landed two Premier League titles, three FA Cups, and a pair of Community Shields with his teammates. In addition, he was named to the PFA Premier League Team of the Year for three straight seasons from 2002-03 to 2004-05. After a controversial transfer saga, Cole left for fellow London rivals Chelsea in the summer of 2006.

9. Kenny Sansom may not have received the same fanfare as some of his fellow Arsenal defenders, but he was a steady presence with the club at left-back between 1980 and 1988. He served as captain in 1986-1987 and helped the side hoist the League Cup in 1987. Sansom was Arsenal player of the year for 1981 and made 394 appearances before joining Newcastle United in December 1988. With 86 England caps to his name, Sansom is his nation's second most-capped fullback behind the great Bobby Moore.

10. Left-back Nigel Winterburn served Arsenal from 1987 to 2000 and got into 584 games and also played a couple of times with England. The defensive specialist managed to chip in with the odd goal when he'd attack down the flank and he left Arsenal with numerous team medals. Winterburn aided his squad in winning three league titles, two FA Cups, a League Cup, three Charity Shields, and a European Cup Winners' Cup. He left for West Ham United in 2000 and entered the world of coaching and broadcasting after retiring three years later.

CHAPTER 6:

MAESTROS OF THE MIDFIELD

QUIZ TIME!

1. Which midfielder scored 59 goals for Arsenal?

    a. Liam Brady

    b. George Armstrong

    c. David Jack

    d. Jimmy Logie

2. Bob John made more than 460 appearances for the club.

    a. True

    b. False

3. Paul Merson led the club with how many assists in the 1992-93 Premier League?

    a. 7

    b. 8

    c. 9

    d. 10

4. Which attacking midfielder scored 18 goals in all competitions in 2003-04?

   a. Edu Gaspar
   b. Patrick Vieira
   c. Freddie Ljungberg
   d. Robert Pirès

5. Who led the club with 11 assists in all competitions in 2019-20?

   a. Nicolas Pépé
   b. Mesut Özil
   c. Granit Xhaka
   d. Bukayo Saka

6. How many assists did Cesc Fàbregas record in the 2009-10 Premier League?

   a. 10
   b. 13
   c. 14
   d. 16

7. Marc Overmars scored 16 goals in his first season with the club in all competitions.

   a. True
   b. False

8. Who bolstered his team with 20 assists in all competitions in 2015-16?

   a. Alexis Sánchez
   b. Theo Walcott

c. Mesut Özil

d. Aaron Ramsey

9. Which midfielder played 2,639 minutes in 2010-11 domestic league matches?

   a. Jack Wilshere
   b. Alex Song
   c. Samir Nasri
   d. Andrey Arshavin

10. How old was Liam Brady when he made his professional debut with Arsenal in 1973?

    a. 16
    b. 17
    c. 18
    d. 19

11. Whose only goal for Arsenal came from the penalty spot in a shootout during the 2013-14 FA Cup semifinal?

    a. Chuba Akpom
    b. Kim Källström
    c. Ryo Miyaichi
    d. Serge Gnabry

12. Midfielder David Rocastle's eyesight was so poor he could not see the goal from half-field. after the club fitted him with contact lenses, his play improved.

    a. True
    b. False

13. Which midfielder tallied 12 goals and 11 assists in his debut campaign for Arsenal in 2012-13?

   a. Gervinho
   b. Alex Oxlade-Chamberlain
   c. Serge Gnabry
   d. Santi Cazorla

14. Which midfielder completed 1,656 passes in 2019-20 domestic league matches?

   a. Lucas Torreria
   b. Dani Ceballos
   c. Granit Xhaka
   d. Mattéo Guendouzi

15. In 2012-13, Mikel Arteta attempted 6 penalty kicks and scored on how many of them?

   a. 3
   b. 4
   c. 5
   d. 6

16. Patrick Vieira was shown 75 yellow cards during his nine years with Arsenal.

   a. True
   b. False

17. Who was the only midfielder to be shown a red card in the 2006-07 season?

   a. Gilberto Silva
   b. Tomáš Rosický

c. Alexander Hleb

d. Mathieu Flamini

18. How many assists did Alex Song have in the 2011-12 Premier League?

a. 8

b. 6

c. 14

d. 10

19. In 1995-96, which midfielder played the most minutes?

a. David Platt

b. Paul Merson

c. Ray Parlour

d. Glenn Helder

20. Between the 2017 and 2020 Premier League seasons, Granit Xhaka has been shown 43 yellow cards.

a. True

b. False

QUIZ ANSWERS

1. A – Liam Brady

2. A – True

3. C – 9

4. D – Robert Pirès

5. D – Bukayo Saka

6. B – 13

7. A – True

8. C – Mesut Özil

9. A – Jack Wilshere

10. B – 17

11. B – Kim Källström

12. A – True

13. D – Santi Cazorla

14. C – Granit Xhaka

15. C – 5

16. A – True

17. A – Gilberto Silva

18. D – 10

19. B – Paul Merson

20. B – False

DID YOU KNOW?

1. French international Robert Pirès had already won the World Cup and European Championship when he joined the Gunners in his prime from Marseille in 2000. He spent the next six seasons with the team, scoring more than 80 goals in just under 300 contests. He featured heavily on the left side as Arsenal won two league titles and FA Cups during his stay and reached the final of the 2005-06 European Champions League. He notched 14 league goals for three straight seasons from 2002-03 to 2004-2005 and was named FWA Footballer of the Year for 2001–02. He was also named to the PFA Premier League Team of the Year for three consecutive seasons from 2001–02 to 2003-04.

2. Former Arsenal youth player Liam Brady went on to become one of the club's best all-round midfielders between 1973 and 1980. Known for his passing, playmaking, vision, and dribbling skills, the Republic of Ireland international also chipped in with 59 goals in 307 games. He was a regular by the time he was 18 years old and formed an excellent midfield partnership with Allan Ball. Brady helped the team win the FA Cup in 1979 and was named PFA Player of the Season that year. Brady was also named Arsenal Player of the Year for 1977, 1978, and 1979 and made the PFA Team of the Year for three straight campaigns from 1977-78 to 1979-80. Brady's side lost the

1979-80 Cup Winners' Cup Final in a penalty shootout to Valencia after beating Juventus in the semifinal. Brady was so impressive that Juventus paid approximately £500,000 for him just months later.

3. Jack Wilshere was just 16 years and 256 days old when he made his Gunners' debut in September 2008, making him the youngest first-team player in club history at the time. He notched his first goal for the club in a League Cup outing 10 days later and his fine performances eventually led to a call up to England's national side. After suffering several injuries, Arsenal gave up on the former academy player in June 2018 when he left for West Ham United. Wilshere managed to play just under 200 times with the squad in a decade while being awarded the BBC Premier League goal of the season in 2013-14 and 2014-15. He was also named the 2010-11 PFA Young Player of the Year and Arsenal Player of the Season as well as being named to the PFA Team of the Year.

4. There's no doubt Patrick Vieira is one of the Premier League's all-time midfield greats and he's also arguably the best of the Arsenal bunch. Vieira became a legend with the Gunners as he displayed a tremendous desire to win at all costs. He didn't back down from anybody and the incredibly talented French international player captained the squad for three of his nine seasons at Arsenal. He was a key member of the Invincibles side that went undefeated in 2003-04 and was named to the Premier League Team of the Season six times. Vieira helped the Gunners win three

league titles and four FA Cups in just over 400 appearances before leaving for Juventus in 2005.

5. As of 2021, Alan Ball was just one of several English internationals who won a World Cup winner's medal in 1966. He didn't join Arsenal until December 1971 when he was bought for a then club-record fee of £220,000. Ball helped the side reach the 1972 FA Cup final but wasn't able to add another medal to his collection. He did manage to score 52 goals in just over 200 appearances though before leaving for Southampton in December 1976. Ball also served as the Gunners' captain between 1974 and 1976 when he was healthy.

6. One of Arsenal's earliest midfield workhorses was Roddy McEachrane of Scotland, who moved to London as a 20-year-old to work and play football at the Thames Iron Works. The strong-tackling midfielder helped the team capture the 1898-99 Southern League Division Two championship and played over 100 games with them until 1902. McEachrane then joined Woolwich Arsenal and helped them earn promotion to the First Division of the Football League in 1904. However, they were relegated in 1912-13, which proved to be McEachrane's last season. It's believed he played 346 games with Arsenal but never scored a goal or won a cup or league medal.

7. Paul Davis was an unsung hero with Arsenal between 1980 and 1995, scoring 37 goals in just under 450 appearances. He was an excellent passer with great vision

who helped the club claim two league and League Cup titles along with an FA Cup, European Cup Winners' Cup, Charity Shield, and the Football League Centenary Trophy in 1988. After leaving Arsenal, he went to Norway to play but returned to the club in 1996 to become a youth coach and later joined the English FA to work with the elite coach development team.

8. Another early Gunners' midfield presence was Englishman Alf Baker, who also filled in at right-back when needed. Baker, who was a miner before becoming a pro footballer, played for several amateur teams before signing with Arsenal in 1919. Nicknamed "Doughy," Baker could play any position and even took over in goal during emergencies. However, he was generally seen on the right side of the pitch as a midfielder and was team captain in 1924-25. Baker played in the Gunners' first FA Cup final in 1927 and helped them win the trophy for the first time in 1930. He retired in 1931 after playing over 350 games and later became a scout with the team.

9. When Cesc Fàbregas showed up at the Emirates Stadium from Barcelona he was just 16 years old, but it didn't take him long to become one of the club's best-ever playmaking midfielders and a key Spanish international. In 2003, he became the club's youngest first-team player at the age of 16 years and 177 days and soon became its youngest goal-scorer when he tallied in the League Cup. Fàbregas was named team captain at the age of 21 in 2008. His stay in London was relatively short, though, as he appeared in

just over 300 games while scoring 57 goals. Fàbregas returned to Barcelona in the summer of 2011 but not before helping the Gunners win the 2004 Community Shield and the 2005 FA Cup.

10. Freddie Ljungberg, who managed Arsenal for a brief time in 2019, was another important member of the 2003-04 Invincibles side. The Swedish international had speed to burn and the offensive skills to contribute 72 goals in just over 320 outings. He joined the Gunners as a 21-year-old in 1998 and remained until July 2007. He won the Premier League and FA Cup double in 2001-02 along with another league title and two more FA Cups. Ljungberg, who was named Premier League Player of the Season for 2001-02, returned to the Gunners in 2013 as an ambassador and again in 2018 as a coach before saying goodbye in 2020.

CHAPTER 7:

SENSATIONAL STRIKERS/FORWARDS

QUIZ TIME!

1. Who led Arsenal with 15 goals in the 1992-93 Premier League?

    a. Paul Dickov

    b. Alan Smith

    c. Kevin Campbell

    d. Ian Wright

2. Thierry Henry scored only 7 goals his first season with Arsenal.

    a. True

    b. False

3. In 2008-09, Robin van Persie led the club in assists, recording how many in the Premier League?

    a. 9

    b. 10

    c. 11

    d. 12

4. Which forward made over 480 appearances for the Gunners?

   a. John Radford
   b. Dennis Bergkamp
   c. Thierry Henry
   d. Cliff Bastin

5. Which forward scored the winning goal in extra time of the FA Cup final to secure Arsenal's first double in 1971?

   a. Ray Kennedy
   b. George Armstrong
   c. Charlie George
   d. John Radford

6. How many goals did Pierre-Emerick Aubameyang score in the 2019-20 Premier League?

   a. 17
   b. 19
   c. 21
   d. 22

7. Ian Wright scored a hat trick in his Arsenal debut against Leicester City in the 1991 League Cup.

   a. True
   b. False

8. Which forward scored 24 goals in all competitions in 2015-16?

   a. Olivier Giroud
   b. Alexis Sánchez

c. Alex Iwobi

d. Chris Willock

9. Which player received a total of 8 yellow cards in 1999-2000?

a. Thierry Henry

b. Nwankwo Kanu

c. Dennis Bergkamp

d. Davor Šuker

10. Alexis Sánchez scored how many domestic league goals in 2014-15?

a. 14

b. 16

c. 18

d. 20

11. How many assists did Alexandre Lacazette record in the 2018-19 Premier League?

a. 7

b. 8

c. 9

d. 10

12. Dennis Bergkamp was the first Dutch player inducted into the English Football Hall of Fame.

a. True

b. False

13. Who scored on all three of his penalty kicks in the 2007-08 Premier League?

a. Nicklas Bendtner

b. Robin van Persie

c. Eduardo da Silva

d. Emmanuel Adebayor

14. Where does Ian Wright rank in the all-time scoring list for the club?

a. 5th

b. 4th

c. 3rd

d. 2nd

15. How many appearances did Thierry Henry make for the club?

a. 377

b. 396

c. 347

d. 400

16. Thierry Henry scored over 40 goals in all competitions in 2003-04.

a. True

b. False

17. On Dec. 14, 1935, Ted Drake had a game to remember, scoring a then-record 7 goals against which club?

a. Grimsby Town

b. Nottingham Forrest

c. Aston Villa

d. Chelsea

18. Which forward scored 116 goals in 176 matches between 1935 and 1953?

    a. Jack Lambert

    b. Ray Bowden

    c. Alf Kirchen

    d. Reg Lewis

19. How many goals did Alan Smith score in the first league match of the 1988-89 season?

    a. 1

    b. 2

    c. 3

    d. 4

20. In his best season with Arsenal, Robin van Persie scored over 30 goals in all competitions in 2011-12.

    a. True

    b. False

QUIZ ANSWERS

1. D – Ian Wright

2. B – False

3. B – 10

4. A – John Radford

5. C – Charlie George

6. D – 22

7. B – False

8. A – Olivier Giroud

9. C – Dennis Bergkamp

10. B – 16

11. B – 8

12. A – True

13. D – Emmanuel Adebayor

14. D – 2nd

15. A – 377

16. B – False

17. C – Aston Villa

18. D – Reg Lewis

19. C – 3

20. A – True

DID YOU KNOW?

1. Classy Dutch international Dennis Bergkamp came to Arsenal from Inter Milan in 1995 and thrilled Gunners' fans with his sublime goals and playmaking abilities. He notched 120 goals in just over 420 games, with many of them being quite remarkable. Bergkamp, who had a fear of flying, helped his side capture three league titles, FA Cups, and Charity/Community Shields. He was named to the 1997-98 PFA Premier League Team of the Year and was also awarded the FWA Footballer of the Year and PFA Players' Player of the Year honors the same season while winning the BBC Goal of the Season award for 1997–98 and 2001–02. Bergkamp finished his career with the Gunners and is honored by a statue outside of Emirates Stadium.

2. Center-forward Reg Lewis spent his entire career with Arsenal from 1938 to 1953 and contributed more than 115 goals in a little more than 170 appearances. He joined as a schoolboy and scored on his debut in January 1938. The Gunners won the League that season but the youngster wasn't eligible for a medal because he played just four games. After breaking into the squad in 1938-39, his career was interrupted by World War II, when no official games were recorded. After the war, Lewis cemented himself as a regular and helped the team to the league title in 1948-49 and the FA Cup in 1950, when he scored both goals in a 2-0 triumph over Liverpool.

3. Young Frank Stapleton started his pro career with the Gunners in 1974, having arrived two years earlier as an apprentice. He remained until 1981, when he was sold to Manchester United. During his Arsenal stay, Stapleton chipped in with 108 goals in 300 outings. The Republic of Ireland international helped the team reach three FA Cup Finals and winning the trophy in 1979. Stapleton led his squad in scoring for three straight seasons. A great header of the ball, Stapleton would later manage in the North American MLS league.

4. Theo Walcott was another young Gunner who registered 108 goals for the club as he played up front from 2006 to 2018. The speedy England international was bought from Southampton in 2006 and played both as a winger and striker. In May, Walcott became the youngest English international ever when he was 17 years and 75 days old and later he became the youngest England player to score a hat trick for the team. He left for Everton in January 2018 after helping Arsenal win a pair of FA Cups and Community Shields.

5. With an even 100 goals in 156 games, Joe Baker was one of the Gunners' most prolific forwards. He joined the team in 1962 for a then club-record fee of £70,000 from Torino in Italy. He played four seasons with Arsenal and led the squad in scoring in three of them. He was a dynamic attacker due to his pace and aerial ability and he formed an excellent striking partnership with Geoff Strong. Because he was born in Liverpool, Baker was eligible to

play internationally only for England at the time even though he played for Hibernian in Scotland early in his career and had lived most of his life there. In 1959, Baker became the first Scottish League player to play for England and the first pro player to play for the country while playing for a non-English club.

6. While he was best known as Arsenal manager for several years, George Graham was also a useful forward/midfielder for the club in earlier years. Manager Bertie Mee paid £50,000 to Chelsea for him in 1966 and also gave up Tommy Baldwin. Graham led the Gunners in scoring in 1966-67 and 1967-68 as a center-forward and helped his team reach the League Cup final in both 1968 and 1969. He eventually won a medal in 1969-70 when Arsenal won the Inter-Cities Fairs Cup and followed up by capturing the 1970–71 League and FA Cup double. The Scottish international scored 77 goals in just over 300 games with Arsenal before being sold to Manchester United for £120,000 in December 1972.

7. George "Geordie" Armstrong played on the Arsenal wing 621 times between 1962 and 1977, with 500 of those games coming in league action, and he pulled his weight by chipping in with 68 goals. Armstrong was just 17 years old when he made his debut and, by the time he left the club for Leicester City, he held the club record for most appearances. After hanging up his boots, Armstrong entered the world of football management and at one time served as boss of the Kuwait national team. He then

returned to the Gunners in 1990 as a reserve-team coach until passing away in 2000. He helped the club win the Inter-Cities Fairs Cup in 1970 and the League and FA Cup double in 1970-71. He was named the team's player of the year in 1970.

8. Known as 'Supermac," forward Malcolm Macdonald had made quite a name for himself with Fulham, Luton Town, and Newcastle United by the time Arsenal bought him in 1976 from Newcastle for the odd fee of £333,333.34. They knew he could score as he won the Golden Boot with Newcastle in 1974-75 with 21 goals and he added another 57 in just over 100 matches with the Gunners. Twenty-five of those goals came in 1976-77 league action, when Macdonald won his second Golden Boot. The English international played just four times in 1978-79 due to a knee injury and soon retired to dabble in management and broadcasting.

9. Scottish international forward Charlie Nicholas displayed his scoring prowess with Glasgow Celtic by notching 48 goals in 74 games, which led Arsenal to buy him for £750,000 in June 1983. He spent just over four years with the Gunners and posted 54 goals in a little over 180 contests. He scored both goals in the Gunners 1987 League Cup Final victory over Liverpool. Nicknamed "Champagne Charlie" while in London for his love of the nightlife, Nicholas fell out of favor with Arsenal and was sold to Aberdeen in January 1988 for £400,000.

10. John "Jack" Lambert was a big English center-forward who was signed in 1926 by manager Herbert Chapman. Lambert scored just four goals in his first 32 games then broke loose with 18 goals in his next 20 league outings along with four goals in six FA Cup matches. He helped the team win the 1932 FA Cup as well as two league titles and Charity Shields. He netted 38 goals in 34 league matches in 1930-31 to set a club record at the time with seven hat tricks that season as the team won its first League title. Lambert was sold to Fulham in 1933 after scoring 109 times for Arsenal in 161 games with a dozen hat tricks. He returned to the Gunners as a coach in 1938 and sadly passed away in December 1940 at the age of 38 from an automobile accident.

CHAPTER 8:

NOTABLE TRANSFERS/SIGNINGS

QUIZ TIME!

1. Which player did Arsenal sign from Real Madrid for a reported £42 million in 2013?

    a. Mathieu Flamini

    b. Mesut Özil

    c. Santi Cazorla

    d. Nacho Monreal

2. Arsenal acquired Robin van Persie from Dutch club FC Twente.

    a. True

    b. False

3. How much did Arsenal spend to sign Nicolas Pépé from French squad Lille in 2019?

    a. Approximately £45 million

    b. Approximately £50 million

    c. Approximately £65 million

    d. Approximately £72 million

4. Whom did Arsenal transfer to German club Werder Bremen for approximately £4 million in 2016-17?

    a. Mikel Arteta
    b. Mathieu Flamini
    c. Serge Gnabry
    d. Tomáš Rosický

5. Which Italian club did Arsenal sell Gervinho to in 2013-14 for a fee of £8 million?

    a. Inter Milan
    b. Genoa
    c. AS Roma
    d. S.S. Lazio

6. Which of these players was not acquired in the 2003-04 transfer window?

    a. Gilberto Silva
    b. Cesc Fàbregas
    c. Jens Lehmann
    d. Robin van Persie

7. Midfielder Thomas Partey was bought for a reported £45 million from Atletico Madrid in October 2020.

    a. True
    b. False

8. Which player was signed for approximately £1.8 million in the 2010-11 season and played just one league match?

    a. Joel Campbell
    b. Park Chu-Young

c. Jon Toral

d. André Santos

9. In 2012, Arsenal sold Robin van Persie to rival club Manchester United for what approximate fee?

   a. £18 million
   b. £20 million
   c. £22 million
   d. £27 million

10. Arsenal acquired Thierry Henry from Juventus in 1999 for a transfer fee of what price?

   a. £8 million
   b. £9 million
   c. £10 million
   d. £11 million

11. In 2005-06, Arsenal transferred which player to Italian club Juventus for a fee of approximately £13 million?

   a. David Bentley
   b. Ashley Cole
   c. Francis Jeffers
   d. Patrick Vieira

12. In 2018-19, Arsenal signed Sokratis Papastathopoulos from Italian club U.C. Sampdoria.

   a. True
   b. False

13. In 1977, Arsenal signed teenaged winger Mark Heeley from which club?

a. Northampton Town

b. Peterborough United

c. Manchester City

d. Toronto Blizzard

14. Which club did Arsenal sell forward Emmanuel Adebayor to in 2009?

a. Manchester United

b. Tottenham Hotspur

c. Chelsea

d. Manchester City

15. Which player did Arsenal sell for a club-record transfer fee of approximately £40 million?

a. Cesc Fàbregas

b. Alex Iwobi

c. Alex Oxlade-Chamberlain

d. Marc Overmars

16. In 2018-19, Arsenal signed keeper Bernd Leno from German club Bayer Leverkusen.

a. True

b. False

17. What was the reported fee that Arsène Wenger sold Samir Nasri to Manchester City for in 2011-12?

a. £18 million

b. £25 million

c. £27 million

d. £29 million

18. What was the approximate fee paid to acquire Robin van Persie in 2004?

    a. £1 million
    b. £2.75 million
    c. £24 million
    d. £35 million

19. In 2015-16, 10 players were transferred out of Arsenal, how many left the club on a free transfer?

    a. 5
    b. 6
    c. 7
    d. 8

20. Arsène Wenger signed Mikel Arteta from fellow Premier League club, Everton, in 2011 for a fee of £10 million.

    a. True
    b. False

QUIZ ANSWERS

1. B – Mesut Özil

2. B – False

3. D – Approximately £72 million

4. C – Serge Gnabry

5. C – AS Roma

6. A – Gilberto Silva

7. A – True

8. B – Park Chu-Young

9. C – £22 million

10. D – £11 million

11. D – Patrick Vieira

12. B - False

13. B – Peterborough United

14. D – Manchester City

15. C – Alex Oxlade-Chamberlain

16. A – True

17. B – £25 million

18. B – £2.75 million

19. D – 8

20. A – True

DID YOU KNOW?

1. French international defender William Gallas handed Chelsea boss José Mourinho a transfer request in 2006 that was promptly rejected. His contract was due to expire the next year and Gallas claimed he wouldn't stay with the organization unless they met his salary demands. Chelsea then released a statement claiming Gallas admitted that he'd score goals on his own team if the club didn't release him. Gallas denied the accusation while calling the club petty and classless. The player was eventually dealt to Arsenal after the Gunners sent fellow defender Ashley Cole the other way. Gallas was handed the Arsenal captaincy soon after but stripped of it two years later. He demanded more money from the Gunners for the 2010-11 campaign after his contract had expired but was refused. He then signed with Tottenham Hotspur.

2. When English international Ashley Cole was shipped from Arsenal to Chelsea for William Gallas, the Gunners also received £5 million. Cole had been reportedly offered £55,000 a week by Arsenal in a new deal, but he wasn't satisfied because Chelsea allegedly offered him £90,000 per week. Cole and his agent then met with Chelsea manager José Mourinho and club CEO Peter Kenyon even though he was still under contract to Arsenal. All the parties present at the June 2005 meeting were fined heavily but, following an appeal, the amounts were reduced. After

meeting with Chelsea, Cole eventually agreed to a one-year extension with Arsenal. Twelve months later, Cole criticized Arsenal in his autobiography and the club left him out of its 2006-07 team photo before sending him to Chelsea in August 2006.

3. Sol Campbell was another English international defender who departed one London rival for another when he bolted from Tottenham Hotspur to join Arsenal in 2001. Campbell, who was Tottenham captain, was free to move because his contract was about to expire. He was offered a new deal that would have made him the highest-paid player in Spurs' history and Campbell publicly stated that he intended to stay at White Hart Lane. However, he inked a deal with Arsenal and, to make matters worse for Tottenham and their fans, the club didn't receive a thing since it was a free transfer. Campbell, who said he joined the Gunners to play Champions League football, received all types of abuse from many Tottenham supporters following the move as they branded him a traitor.

4. Arsenal manager Arsène Wenger signed injury-prone French midfielder Amaury Bischoff from Werder Bremen in Germany in the summer of 2008 but things didn't work out too well. Bischoff managed to play just 26 minutes of Premier League football when he came on as a substitute for Theo Walcott in his only appearance in May 2009. The only other action he saw was as a substitute in three domestic cup matches and he was released from the club in June 2009, when his contract was up.

5. One of the most expensive teenage signings in Premier League history involved winger/midfielder Alex Oxlade-Chamberlain. Arsenal paid Southampton a reported £12 million for him in August 2011, when he was just 17 years old. The English international scored 20 times in 198 games with the Gunners before being sold to Liverpool in 2017 for a reported £35 million fee. Oxlade-Chamberlain became the youngest Englishman to score in the UEFA Champions League and helped the Gunners win three FA Cups and Community Shields. Oxlade-Chamberlain has unfortunately been injury-prone during his career and was still with Liverpool as of January 2021.

6. Another huge teenage transfer involved Arsenal buying from Southampton as the club paid a reported £16 million in the summer of 2014 for 19-year-old defender Calum Chambers. He was loaned to Middlesbrough for most of the 2016-17 season and was with Fulham for 2018-19, where he was named the team's player of the year. He returned to the Gunners in 2019 and then tore his ACL in December. Chambers returned to the pitch in 2021 and, as of January 2021, had played just over 100 games with the club and had earned three caps for England.

7. Not all transfers work out well; striker Francis Jeffers is an example. Jeffers had impressed on the pitch at Everton from 1997 to 2001 with 18 goals in 49 league outings and he also scored 13 times in 16 games with the England Under-21 side. Arsenal paid £8 million for his services in June 2001. However, he managed to score just four times

in 22 contests with the Gunners before being shipped back on loan to Everton in 2003-04. He then drifted around the UK, playing for numerous other sides before playing in Australia and Malta. Jeffers wound up with Accrington Stanley in 2013 before retiring at the age of 32 and turning to coaching.

8. Another young prospect who failed to live up to his potential was teenager Mark Heeley, who was signed from Peterborough United in September 1977 for £50,000. The winger was Peterborough's youngest-ever first-team player at 16 and looked to be a future star even though he played just 17 times with the club, scoring 3 goals. The Gunners played the youngster in Europe and in the league, but he appeared in just 15 games and scored once. Heeley appeared to have lost his passion for the game and was sold to Northampton Town in March 1980 for £35,000. He ended up with several non-league teams and then hung up his boots well before turning 25 years old.

9. Trades are a rarity in English soccer, but Arsenal was involved in what turned out to be a major one in the summer of 1980. The Gunners bid £1 million to Crystal Palace for defender Kenny Sansom and also included striker Clive Allen in the package. This was deemed a bit odd since Allen had been acquired by Arsenal for £125 million just a few weeks earlier from Queens Park Rangers, where he had scored 32 goals in 29 games. Allen finished his career with just over 240 goals and he won the 1986-87 PFA Player of the Year and Football Writers'

Association Footballer of the Year Awards. Sansom also enjoyed an excellent career but one wonders how things would have turned out if Arsenal simply paid cash for Sansom while also keeping Allen.

10. As of January 2021, Arsenal's biggest transfer payment was reportedly the club-record £72 million paid to Lille of France in August 2019 for French international forward Nicolas Pépé. The jury's still out on him, though, as he repaid the club with 8 goals in 42 appearances in 2019-20 while helping the side win the 2020 FA Cup. He then notched 5 goals in his first 20 appearances in 2020-21 for a total of 13 goals in 62 games with the Gunners. Pépé will turn 26 years old on May 29, 2021, so there's still plenty of time for debate.

CHAPTER 9:

ODDS & ENDS

QUIZ TIME!

1. What was the South Stand of Arsenal's Highbury Stadium nicknamed?

   a. The Cannon's Rest
   b. The Clock End
   c. The Clock Tower
   d. The Armoury

2. In 1919, Arsenal was controversially promoted to the First Division by a vote instead of Tottenham Hotspur, fueling their rivalry in the process.

   a. True
   b. False

3. How many Arsenal players were in the lineup of England's national team for the infamous "Battle of Highbury" in 1934?

   a. 4
   b. 5

c. 6

d. 7

4. In Arsenal's first season in the Football League (1893-94), how many matches did they win?

   a. 9

   b. 10

   c. 11

   d. 12

5. In 1931, Arsenal beat which team 9-1 at Highbury?

   a. Blackpool

   b. Newcastle United

   c. Grimsby Town

   d. Derby County

6. What is the most goals Arsenal has conceded in a season during the Premier League era?

   a. 38

   b. 42

   c. 49

   d. 51

7. In the 2003-04 season, Arsenal became the first club of the Premier League era to not lose a single league match.

   a. True

   b. False

8. When Arsenal was relegated in 1912-13, the club only won how many of its 38 games?

a. 2

b. 3

c. 4

d. 5

9. Who was the first Gunners' player to be sent off at the Emirates Stadium in a match against Portsmouth on Sept. 2, 2007?

a. Mathieu Flamini

b. Abou Diaby

c. Nicklas Bendtner

d. Philippe Senderos

10. What was the Arsenal squad nicknamed after their historical 2003-04 season in which they went undefeated?

a. The Perfection Squad

b. The Kings' Men

c. The Invincibles

d. The Unbeatables

11. The 1970-71 campaign proved to be the club's best season, ending with how many domestic league wins?

a. 25

b. 27

c. 29

d. 32

12. On April 21, 1930, Arsenal's highest-scoring draw came against Leicester City with a final score of 6-6.

a. True

b. False

13. In August 2011, Arsenal lost 8-2 to set a personal record for most goals conceded in a Premier League match against which club?

    a. Chelsea
    b. Manchester United
    c. Liverpool
    d. Manchester City

14. Which player made 172 consecutive appearances for the team?

    a. David O'Leary
    b. Tom Parker
    c. Robin van Persie
    d. David Seaman

15. What is the highest number of matches Arsenal has drawn in a single season as of 2020?

    a. 14
    b. 17
    c. 18
    d. 20

16. Starting on May 24, 2007, Arsenal went 12 consecutive games without a win at Emirates Stadium.

    a. True
    b. False

17. In 2004-05, the squad set a club record in the Premier League era by scoring how many goals?

    a. 87
    b. 88

c. 90

d. 92

18. Who was the oldest player to make an appearance for Arsenal at the age of 41 years and 159 days old?

a. Jock Rutherford

b. Jens Lehmann

c. John Lukic

d. Mikel Arteta

19. How many points did Arsenal secure on the league table in their 2003-04 season?

a. 87

b. 88

c. 89

d. 90

20. The Gunners drew 14 games in the 2003-04 Premier League season.

a. True

b. False

QUIZ ANSWERS

1. B – The Clock End

2. A – True

3. D – 7

4. D – 12

5. C – Grimsby Town

6. D – 51

7. A – True

8. B – 3

9. D – Philippe Senderos

10. C – The Invincibles

11. C – 29

12. A – True

13. B – Manchester United

14. B – Tom Parker

15. C – 18

16. B – False

17. A – 87

18. A – Jock Rutherford

19. D – 90

20. B – False

DID YOU KNOW?

1. Kroenke Sports & Entertainment, who currently owns the Arsenal club with over 90 percent of the shares, also owns several other media outlets, properties, stadiums, and sports franchises. These include the Los Angeles Rams (NFL), the Denver Nuggets (NBA), the Colorado Avalanche (NHL), the Colorado Rapids (MLS), the Colorado Mammoth (NLL), the Los Angeles Gladiators (OWL), and the Los Angeles Guerrillas (CDL).

2. In 1932, the Gillespie Road underground station, on the London Piccadilly Line between the Finsbury Park and Holloway Road stations, was renamed Arsenal Station after the football club, which at that time was playing its home games at the nearby Arsenal (Highbury) Stadium. This is currently the only underground rail station in England named directly after a football club.

3. Arsenal (Highbury) Stadium was overhauled in the 1930s with the additions of new East and Art Deco West stands being built and a roof being added over the North Bank terrace. The roof was damaged during World War II bombing attacks and wasn't fully restored until 1954. Highbury held over 60,000 fans at one time but, when it was converted to an all-seat stadium for 1993–94, the capacity was reduced to 38,419. Therefore, the club played home European Champions League games at London's Wembley Stadium between 1998 and 2000.

4. As of January 2021, Arsenal's record home attendance stands at 73,707, which was set at Wembley Stadium in November 1998 for a European Champions League game with RC Lens. The largest crowd for a home game at Arsenal (Highbury) Stadium came in March 1935 in a 0-0 draw with Sunderland, when 73,295 fans were on hand. The current largest gathering for a home match at Emirates Stadium was for a 2-2 draw against Manchester United in November 2007, when there were 60,161 in the stands.

5. The Emirates Stadium, which is approximately 500 meters southwest of the old Arsenal (Highbury) Stadium, was finished in July 2006. It's named after Emirates Airline, which sponsors the ground for a reported £100 million until at least 2028. In addition, the airline will sponsor the club's shirts until at least 2024. The stands at the Emirates Stadium were officially named North Bank, East Stand, West Stand, and the Clock End in 2010.

6. The Arsenal squad has been training at the Shenley Training Centre in Hertfordshire since it opened in 1999. Before that, the players trained at a nearby location that was owned by the University College of London Students' Union. Up until 1961, they trained at Arsenal (Highbury) Stadium. In addition, the Arsenal Academy under-18 sides play home games at Shenley and the reserves play at Meadow Park, which is the home ground of Boreham Wood FC. On some occasions, the under-18 and reserve squads play at the Emirates.

7. Arsenal's greatest and longest rivalry is with their neighbors Tottenham Hotspur, with the rivalry known as the North London derby. The club has other natural rivalries with fellow London-based sides including West Ham United, Fulham, Crystal Palace, Queens Park Rangers, and Chelsea. The Gunners also currently have a strong rivalry with Manchester United with a few on- and off-pitch incidents fueling the flames between the teams.

8. The first English league soccer game to be broadcast live on radio was between Arsenal and Sheffield United from Arsenal (Highbury) Stadium on Jan. 22, 1927. Ten years later, on Sept. 16, 1937, a friendly contest between Arsenal and the reserve side was the first soccer game in the world to be shown live on television. In addition, the very first BBC Match of the Day program featured Arsenal at Liverpool on Aug. 22, 1964, and the first 3D sports event to be televised live publicly featured Arsenal vs Manchester United in January 2010. Also, in August 1928, Arsenal and Chelsea became the first soccer teams to wear numbers on their shirts.

9. Like many pro sports franchises, Arsenal has a club mascot, a green 7-foot-tall dinosaur known as Gunnersaurus Rex. The mascot was first introduced in a home contest against Manchester City in the early 1990s and is based on a contest-winning drawing of a young fan named Peter Lovell. The mascot attends both Arsenal men's and women's home matches as well as numerous community functions.

10. The youngest player to suit up in a first-team match for Arsenal was Cesc Fàbregas at the age of 16 years, 177 days, when he took to the pitch against Rotherham United in the third round of the League Cup in October 2003. The oldest was Jock Rutherford, who was 41 years and 159 days of age in a First Division match against Manchester City in March 1926. Fàbregas and Rutherford were also the youngest and oldest to score a goal for the club.

CHAPTER 10:

DOMESTIC COMPETITION

QUIZ TIME!

1. What was the first domestic cup the club won in 1889-90?

    a. London Charity Cup

    b. Kent Senior Cup

    c. London Senior Cup

    d. London Challenge Cup

2. Arsenal has the record for most FA Cup championships in England.

    a. True

    b. False

3. What year did Arsenal win their first league title?

    a. 1929-30

    b. 1930-31

    c. 1931-32

    d. 1932-33

4. Arsenal defeated which team 2-0 to win its first FA Cup in 1929-30?

a. Manchester City

b. Derby County

c. Sheffield Wednesday

d. Huddersfield Town

5. How many times has Arsenal won the FA Cup as of 2020?

    a. 12

    b. 13

    c. 14

    d. 15

6. How many times has Arsenal won the FA Charity Shield/Community Shield as of 2020?

    a. 16

    b. 12

    c. 18

    d. 14

7. Arsenal has won the top-flight league title 11 times as of 2020.

    a. True

    b. False

8. Which club did Arsenal beat to win their first FA Cup of the Premier League era in 1993?

    a. Sheffield Wednesday

    b. Ipswich Town

    c. Coventry City

    d. Everton

9. How many times has the club won the League Cup (Carabao Cup) as of 2020?

    a. 4
    b. 3
    c. 2
    d. 1

10. Arsenal defeated which club to win their 14th FA Cup final in 2020?

    a. Manchester United
    b. Chelsea
    c. Liverpool
    d. Tottenham Hotspur

11. In 1991, Arsenal shared the honor of the FA Community Shield with which other club?

    a. Chelsea
    b. Manchester United
    c. Tottenham Hotspur
    d. Liverpool

12. Arsenal has beaten Chelsea three times in the FA Cup final as of 2020.

    a. True
    b. False

13. How many times has Arsenal been runners-up in the top-flight division as of 2020?

    a. 8
    b. 11

c. 7

d. 9

14. In 1988-89, Arsenal won the Football Alliance Centenary Trophy, defeating which team 2-1?

    a. Queens Park Rangers
    b. Newcastle United
    c. Manchester United
    d. Wimbledon

15. How many times has Arsenal been runners-up to the FA Cup title as of 2020?

    a. 5
    b. 6
    c. 7
    d. 8

16. Arsenal won the 1903-04 Second Division league title.

    a. True
    b. False

17. Which club did Arsenal defeat 2-1 to win their first League Cup (Carabao Cup) in 1986-87?

    a. Liverpool
    b. Chelsea
    c. Tottenham Hotspur
    d. Aston Villa

18. How many times did the club win the London Challenge Cup?

a. 8

b. 9

c. 10

d. 11

19. As of 2020, how many times has Arsenal secured a domestic FA Cup and League Double?

a. 5

b. 4

c. 3

d. 2

20. In 1992-93, Arsenal won a cup double, winning both the FA Cup and League Cup.

a. True

b. False

QUIZ ANSWERS

1. B – Kent Senior Cup

2. A – True

3. B – 1930-31

4. D – Huddersfield Town

5. C – 14

6. A – 16

7. B – False

8. A – Sheffield Wednesday

9. C – 2

10. B – Chelsea

11. C – Tottenham Hotspur

12. A – True

13. D – 9

14. C – Manchester United

15. C – 7

16. B – False

17. A – Liverpool

18. D – 11

19. B – 4

20. A – True

DID YOU KNOW?

1. January 30, 1965, was a sad day for the UK, as former Prime Minister Winston Churchill was laid to rest. It was also a day most Gunners fans would like to forget because their team traveled about 80 miles north to London Road and fell 2-1 to Peterborough United in the fourth round of the FA Cup. Peterborough, known as "The Posh," was toiling in the Third Division and had joined the Football League just five years earlier while Arsenal was one of the established giants of English soccer. The third-tier side did the unthinkable, though, roaring back from a 1-0 halftime deficit to pull level in the 72nd minute and then notch the winner with five minutes to go.

2. The old First Division was on its last legs in 1992, as the Premier League was launched the next season. There was one more upset to come for Arsenal, though: The reigning league champions visited Wrexham on Jan. 4 and were unceremoniously knocked out of the third round of the FA Cup, 2-1. It couldn't have been more embarrassing for the Gunners because Wrexham was dead last in the Fourth Division at the time. Alan Smith gave Arsenal the lead at the Racecourse Ground in North Wales, but the 37-year-old Mickey Thomas tied the game with eight minutes by drilling home a 25-yard free kick. Steve Watkin then won it for the home side as the last-place team in English pro football knocked off the reigning league champions.

3. Not all was doom and gloom in the FA Cup. Arsenal has won the trophy a record 14 times as of 2020. The Gunners were crowned champions in 1930, 1936, 1950, 1971, 1979, 1993, 1998, 2002, 2003, 2005, 2014, 2015, 2017, and 2020. They also made it to the FA Cup final on seven other occasions but were runners-up in 1927, 1932, 1952, 1972, 1978, 1980, and 2001.

4. Arsenal has also fared well in the FA Charity Shield and Community Shield competitions. This match traditionally launches England's new football season with the trophy typically being contested by the previous season's FA Cup winners and top-flight league champions. Arsenal has won the silverware outright 15 times, in 1930, 1931, 1933, 1934, 1938, 1948, 1953, 1998, 1999, 2002, 2004, 2014, 2015, 2017 and 2020. They shared the trophy in 1991, when they played to a 0-0 draw with Tottenham Hotspur. The Gunners were also runners-up seven times, in 1935, 1936, 1979, 1989, 1993, 2003, and 2005

5. The Gunners certainly haven't been as successful in the Football League Cup. They've won it just twice, in 1987 and 1993. They were also runners-up half a dozen times, in 1968, 1969, 1988, 2007, 2011, and 2018. They did manage to win the 1988 League Centenary Trophy, which was in celebration of the Football League's 100th birthday.

6. The first team to go undefeated in the top tier of English soccer was Preston North End when the First Division side went unbeaten in 1888-89, which was the inaugural

campaign of the professional English Football League. The only other team to achieve the feat was the 2003-04 Arsenal squad, nicknamed "the Invincibles." With Arsène Wenger as manager, the Premier League outfit played 38 league matches that season and posted 26 wins and 12 draws to win the league by 11 points over Chelsea.

7. The 2003-04 unbeaten campaign by the Gunners was especially sweet for the team's supporters because the club clinched the league title against arch-rivals Tottenham Hotspur away at White Hart Lane. Arsenal didn't manage to win anything else that season, however, being eliminated in the semifinals of both the League Cup and FA Cup and they were knocked out of the European Champions League in the quarterfinals. Arsenal managed to extend their league unbeaten streak to an English top-flight record of 49 games the next season until losing 2-0 away to Manchester United in October 2004.

8. Arsenal also holds the English Football League record for scoring at least one goal in 55 straight games from May 19, 2001, to Nov. 30, 2002. In addition, the Gunners hold the league mark for the longest unbeaten streak in away games at 27, from April 5, 2003, to Sept. 25, 2004. The club record for consecutive league victories currently sits at 14 while the most consecutive league defeats is 7. The team record for league games without a win is 23, which was set between September 1912 and March 1913.

9. Arsenal has won 13 league championships as of 2020, all of them in the top flight. This was the First Division until

1992 and the Premier League from then on. The Gunners' title-winning campaigns came in 1930–31, 1932–33, 1933–34, 1934–35, 1937–38, 1947–48, 1952–53, 1970–71, 1988–89, 1990–91, 1997–98, 2001–02, and 2003–04. It was a case of close but no cigar on nine other occasions when they were league runners-up in 1925–26, 1931–32, 1972–73, 1998–99, 1999–2000, 2000–01, 2002–03, 2004–05 and 2015–16. They were also runners-up in the Second Division in 1903–04.

10. Arsenal is often regarded as a defensive side rather than an offensive one but the club has had its fair share of goal-scoring greats. Thierry Henry won the European and Premier League Golden Boot Awards in both 2003-04 and 2004-05, with 30 and 25 goals respectively. He also captured the Premier League Golden Boot in 2001-02 with 24 tallies and in 2005-06 with 27. Other Arsenal greats to earn English top-flight Golden Boots have been Ted Drake (42 goals in 1934-35), Ronnie Rooke (33 goals in 1947-48), Malcolm Macdonald (29 goals in 1976-77-shared), Alan Smith (23 goals in 1988-89 and 22 goals in 1990-91), Ian Wright (26 goals in 1991-92), Robin van Persie (30 goals in 2011-12) and Pierre-Emerick Aubameyang (22 goals in 2018-19-shared). Two of Wright's 26 goals in 1991-92 came with Crystal Palace with the other 24 were scored for Arsenal.

CHAPTER 11:

EUROPE AND BEYOND

QUIZ TIME!

1. What was the first international trophy that Arsenal won?

    a. UEFA Champions League

    b. UEFA Europa League

    c. UEFA Super Cup

    d. Inter-Cities Fairs Cup

2. Arsenal was the first team based in London to appear in a UEFA Champions League final.

    a. True

    b. False

3. Which Italian club defeated Arsenal 2-0 in the 1994 UEFA Super Cup?

    a. AC Milan

    b. Torino FC

    c. Inter Milan

    d. Napoli

4. How many times had Arsenal won the Amsterdam Tournament before it was abolished in 2009?

    a. 2
    b. 3
    c. 4
    d. 5

5. Which team did Arsenal not face in the 1970 Inter-Cities Fairs Cup preliminary rounds?

    a. FC Rouen
    b. Sporting CP
    c. Ajax
    d. Coleraine FC

6. What was the first year Arsenal qualified for the UEFA Champions League?

    a. 1996-97
    b. 1997-98
    c. 1998-99
    d. 1999-00

7. As of 2020, Arsenal has won four major international trophies.

    a. True
    b. False

8. When did Arsenal first compete for the UEFA Cup?

    a. 1977-78
    b. 1978-79
    c. 1979-80
    d. 1980-81

9. Which club defeated the Gunners in the 2005-06 UEFA Champions League final?

   a. FC Barcelona
   b. Villarreal CF
   c. S.L.B. Benfica
   d. Lyon

10. Arsenal faced off against which fellow Premier League club in the 2018-19 UEFA Europa League?

   a. Liverpool
   b. Manchester City
   c. Chelsea
   d. Burnley

11. In the 1979-80 UEFA Cup Winners' Cup, Valencia CF defeated Arsenal, with a final score line of what?

   a. 1-0
   b. 5-4 on penalties
   c. 3-2
   d. 6-5 on penalties

12. Arsenal played against the MLS All-Stars in 2016 and won 2-1.

   a. True
   b. False

13. Who did Arsenal defeat 1-0 in the 1994 UEFA Cup Winners' Cup Final?

   a. Torino FC
   b. Ajax

c. Parma

d. Paris St-Germain

14. In 1989, Arsenal won the Zenith Data Systems Challenge Trophy, an unofficial world championship against which Argentine team?

a. C.A. Independiente

b. Lomas AC

c. Racing Club

d. C.A. River Plate

15. Arsenal faced off against which club in the 1999-00 UEFA Cup Final?

a. Galatasaray S.K

b. Bayer Leverkusen

c. Sturm Graz

d. FC Spartak Moscow

16. Arsenal won the Amsterdam Tournament in its final year of competition.

a. True

b. False

17. What year did Arsenal win its first Saitama City Cup (a pre-season tournament played in Japan)?

a. 2011

b. 2012

c. 2013

d. 2014

18. Arsenal defeated which club 4-3 on aggregate to win the Inter-Cities Fairs Cup in 1970?

    a. Inter Milan
    b. Dinamo Bacău
    c. Valur
    d. R.S.C. Anderlecht

19. How many times has Arsenal been runners-up to the EUFA Cup Winners' Cup as of 2020?

    a. 1
    b. 2
    c. 3
    d. 4

20. Arsenal won the Wembley International Tournament three times in its seven years of existence.

    a. True
    b. False

QUIZ ANSWERS

1. D – Inter-Cities Fairs Cup

2. A – True

3. A – AC Milan

4. B – 3

5. D – Coleraine FC

6. C – 1998-99

7. B – False

8. B – 1978-79

9. A – FC Barcelona

10. C – Chelsea

11. B – 5-4 on penalties

12. A – True

13. C – Parma

14. A – C.A. Independiente

15. A – Galatasaray S.K

16. B – False

17. C – 2013

18. D – R.S.C. Anderlecht

19. B – 2

20. A – True

DID YOU KNOW?

1. For all the glory Arsenal has achieved on its own soil, the club has generally failed to deliver the goods in European competition. The club has never won the European Cup, which became the Champions League in 1992, and has never captured the UEFA Cup, which has been known as the Europa League since 2009. However, the Gunners were runners-up in the Champions League in 2005-06 and in the Europa League in 1999-2000 and 2018-19.

2. Arsenal did manage to win the European Cup Winners' Cup in 1993-94, when they beat Parma of Italy 1-0 in Copenhagen, Denmark, when Alan Smith scored in the 22nd minute. The Gunners were runners-up in 1979-80, when they were downed 5-4 in a penalty shootout by Spanish club Valencia in Brussels, Belgium. The game ended 0-0 after 90 and 120 minutes. In addition, Arsenal lost the 1994-95 final when the tournament's name was changed to the UEFA Cup Winners' Cup. They were edged 2-1 by Zarazoga of Spain in Paris, France. Arsenal fell behind after 67 minutes with John Hartson sending the match into extra time with his goal eight minutes later. However, the Gunners lost in the final minute of extra time.

3. The Gunners' first European success came in 1969-70, when they won the Inter-Cities Fairs Cup, which would

later become the UEFA Cup and then the Europa League. Arsenal lost the first leg of the Final 3-1 away to Anderlecht of Belgium but were 4-3 winners on aggregate after blanking their opponents 3-0 in the second leg at Arsenal (Highbury) Stadium. Ray Kennedy scored in the first leg with Edward Kelly, John Radford, and Jonathon Sammels hitting the back of the net in the second leg.

4. As of 2020, the only other European Final Arsenal has reached was the UEFA Super Cup. This annual game matches the Champions League winners against the Europa League champions. The contest was formerly known as the European Super Cup until being renamed in 1995. Between 1972 and 1999, the Super Cup featured the winners of the European Cup/Champions League against the winners of the UEFA Cup Winners' Cup. It was then played between the Champions League and UEFA Cup victors until the UEFA Cup became the Europa League in 2009. The Gunners were runners-up in 1993-94 after drawing the first leg of the final 0-0 at home against AC Milan of Italy and losing the second leg 2-0 away.

5. Luck wasn't on Arsenal's side in the 2005-06 Champions League Final in Paris, France. The Gunner goalkeeper, Jens Lehmann, was sent off with a red card after just 18 minutes, reducing the side to 10 men for the rest of the match. Lehmann became the first player sent off in a European Cup/Champions League Final when he took Barcelona's Samuel Eto'o down, outside the 18-yard box. Against the odds, Sol Campbell gave the Gunners the lead

in the 37th minute only to see Barcelona score in the 76th and 80th minutes.

6. Arsenal was also down to 10 men against Barcelona in the second leg of a round of-16 Champions League match in Spain in March 2011. With the Gunners up 3-2 on aggregate, Robin van Persie took a shot at net, hoping for a 4-2 lead. However, he was ruled offside by referee Massimo Busacca. To rub salt into the wound, Busacca then showed van Persie a yellow card for allegedly shooting the ball after the whistle had blown. Van Persie claimed he didn't hear a whistle due to the noise being created by the 90,000 fans at the grounds. He was sent off because it was his second yellow card of the game and Barcelona scored twice to advance to the quarterfinals.

7. On the world scene, the Gunners have participated in numerous pre-season and friendly tournaments against clubs from across the globe and have won several of them. However, these aren't official matches. Some of the events Arsenal has won include the Wembley International Tournament, the Amsterdam Tournament, the Malaysia Cup, the Indonesia Cup, the Saitama City Cup, the Premier League Asia Trophy, the MLS All-Star Game, and the Emirates Cup, which the club typically hosts at the Emirates Stadium.

8. As of 2020, Arsenal's record win in European competition was 7–0 against Standard Liège of Belgium in the second round of the UEFA Cup Winners' Cup on Nov. 3, 1993.

They also blanked Slavia Prague of the Czech Republic 7-0 in the group stage of the UEFA Champions League on Oct. 23, 2007.

9. Among the Gunners' record defeats in Europe were a 4-0 loss to AC Milan of Italy in the round of-16 in the UEFA Champions League on Feb. 15, 2012. They were also hammered three times by a score of 5-1 by Bayern Munich of Germany in the Champions League. These defeats took place in the group stage on Nov. 4, 2015, and in the round of-16 on Feb. 15, 2017, and March 7, 2017.

10. Arsenal was the first London-based club to appear in a Champions League Final in 2005-2006. Also, between 1998–99 and 2016–17, they participated in 19 straight Champions League tournaments. Goalkeeper Jens Lehmann posted 10 consecutive clean sheets before losing in the Champions League Final to Barcelona as the club didn't concede a goal in 995 minutes. Thierry Henry played the most European games for the side at 86 and scored the most goals with 42.

CHAPTER 12:

TOP SCORERS

QUIZ TIME!

1. Which player is the all-time leading scorer for Arsenal?

    a. Ian Wright

    b. Cliff Bastin

    c. Thierry Henry

    d. Dennis Bergkamp

2. Thierry Henry once scored 45 goals in a Premier League season.

    a. True

    b. False

3. Which player scored a hat trick in his league debut with the Gunners?

    a. Tony Adams

    b. Robert Pirès

    c. Mark Heeley

    d. Ian Wright

4. Which Arsenal star once scored 7 goals in a top-flight contest?

   a. Ted Drake
   b. Ian Wright
   c. Thierry Henry
   d. Dennis Bergkamp

5. Who was the first player to score 100 goals for the club?

   a. Cliff Bastin
   b. Joe Hulme
   c. David Jack
   d. Jimmy Brain

6. Which player once led the club in scoring for five straight seasons?

   a. Doug Lishman
   b. John Hartson
   c. Santi Cazorla
   d. Aaron Ramsey

7. Robin van Persie won the 2011-12 Premier League Golden Boot with 30 goals.

   a. True
   b. False

8. Which Gunner once scored 34 goals in a season?

   a. Jack Wilshere
   b. Nigel Winterburn
   c. Alexis Sánchez
   d. David Jack

9. How many goals league goals did Alan Smith tally in 1990-91 to win the First Division Golden Boot?

   a. 18
   b. 23
   c. 28
   d. 29

10. Which player notched 22 league goals in 2018/19 to share the Premier League Golden Boot?

   a. Alexandre Lacazette
   b. Danny Welbeck
   c. Pierre-Emerick Aubameyang
   d. Henrikh Mkhitaryan

11. Which player won the 2007-08 Goal of the Season award for his strike against Tottenham Hotspur?

   a. Emmanuel Adebayor
   b. Alexander Hleb
   c. Philippe Senderos
   d. Fabrice Muamba

12. Frank McLintock once led the First Division in scoring.

   a. True
   b. False

13. Which player was credited with scoring 11 goals in European competitions?

   a. Sol Campbell
   b. Doug Lishman
   c. Robin van Persie
   d. John Radford

14. How many goals did Jimmy Brain score in his 232 appearances with the side?

    a. 124
    b. 139
    c. 196
    d. 201

15. Which player was credited with 125 career goals for Arsenal?

    a. Kenny Sansom
    b. Joe Hulme
    c. Charlie George
    d. Malcolm Macdonald

16. Gunners' players have won or shared the top-flight English Golden Boot 12 times as of 2020.

    a. True
    b. False

17. As of 2020, how many different Gunners' players have won or shared the English top-flight Golden Boot?

    a. 4
    b. 6
    c. 8
    d. 10

18. Who scored 33 league goals in 1947-48 to lead the First Division?

    a. Ronnie Rooke
    b. David Jack

c. Bob John

d. Charlie Jones

19. How many league goals did Ted Drake notch in 1934-35 to win the First Division Golden Boot?

    a. 19

    b. 21

    c. 33

    d. 42

20. Thierry Henry won the European Golden Boot three times.

    a. True

    b. False

QUIZ ANSWERS

1. C – Thierry Henry

2. B – False

3. D – Ian Wright

4. A –Ted Drake

5. D – Jimmy Brain

6. A – Doug Lishman

7. A – True

8. D – David Jack

9. B – 23

10. C – Pierre-Emerick Aubemeyang

11. A– Emmanuel Adebayor

12. B – False

13. D – John Radford

14. B – 139

15. B – Joe Hulme

16. A – True

17. C – 8

18. A – Ronnie Rooke

19. D – 42

20. B – False

DID YOU KNOW?

1. Arsenal's all-time leading scorer is French football magician Thierry Henry. The icon started with AS Monaco's youth academy, while Arsène Wenger was the first team manager, and moved to Juventus after winning the 1998 World Cup. Henry joined Arsenal in 1999 and became an exceptional finisher, with 228 goals in 376 appearances, including 175 in the league. The speedy forward won the Premier League Golden Boot four times, along with numerous other individual awards, and he helped his side to two FA Cups, league titles, and Community Shields. He left in 2007 to play with Barcelona but returned to the Gunners on loan from the New York Red Bulls for seven games in January 2012.

2. The beloved Ian Wright earned himself legendary status at Arsenal after arriving in 1991 from London neighbors Crystal Palace, for a club-record fee at the time of £2.5m. He was bought for his scoring prowess and didn't let anybody down, scoring 185 goals in 288 outings before leaving for another London club, West Ham United, in 1998. He scored on his Gunners' debut in the League Cup and notched a hat trick in his league debut with the squad. Wright earned the Golden Boot in his first Arsenal campaign and led the club in goals for six straight seasons. The English international forward helped win two FA Cups a League Cup and the European Cup Winners' Cup.

He's currently the team's second-leading scorer of all time.

3. Nicknamed "The Boy Bastin," English international winger Cliff Bastin poached 178 goals in just under 400 contests to rank third all-time in club scoring. He was first overall from 1939 to 1997, when his record was broken. He joined the outfit in 1929 and remained until retiring in 1947. By the time he turned 19 years old, he had already helped his side win an FA Cup and league title and had earned a cap for England, making him the youngest player to achieve those three feats. Bastin won five league titles and Charity Shields, as well as a pair of FA Cups, with the Gunners.

4. John Radford's Arsenal journey began in 1964 and concluded in 1976 with 149 goals in 481 outings to rank as the team's fourth-leading scorer. The English forward also helped the squad haul in the Inter-Cities Fairs Cup in 1969-70 as well as the League FA Cup double in 1970-71. The hard-working Radford was also a fine playmaker and he became the club's youngest player to notch a hat trick in 1965 when he was still 17 years old. He was eventually sold to West Ham United in December 1976 and later returned to the Emirates Stadium to work as a broadcaster on Arsenal TV.

5. English international center-forward Ted Drake finished his Arsenal career with 139 goals in 184 games to rank tied for fifth on the club's all-time hit parade. He was the first Gunner to win the Golden Boot, with 42 goals in 41 league

outings in 1934-35. He could also score in bunches as Drake enjoyed four 4-goal games that campaign, along with 3 hat tricks. He also added a goal each in the Charity Shield and FA Cup for a total of 44, which is still the club record for goals in a season. He scored a club-record seven times in a game the next season. Drake won two league titles, an FA Cup, and a Charity Shield between 1934 and 1945. He went on to manage Chelsea to their first league championship in 1954-55.

6. With a name like Jimmy Brain, the Arsenal forward must have been great with his head. He was also excellent with his feet. He's currently tied as the fifth-leading scorer in team annals with 139 goals in 239 encounters. He arrived at the club in 1923 and helped the Gunners capture the 1930 Charity Shield and their first league crown in 1930-31. The team also won the FA Cup in 1930, but Brain played just six league matches that campaign due to injury. Brain was the first Arsenal player to reach the 100-goal plateau. He was sold to Tottenham Hotspur in September 1931.

7. Arsenal paid Walsall approximately £10,500 for Doug Lishman in 1948 and he didn't disappoint, registering 137 goals in 244 contests before being sold to Nottingham Forest in 1956. Along the way, the English forward helped the team win the 1950 FA Cup and the league title in 1952-53. He also led the team in scoring for five straight years from 1951 to 1955. He tallied 30 goals in 1951-52, including hat tricks in three consecutive home outings. He added 22 goals the next season and each of them was crucial

because the Gunners won the league on goal difference over Preston North End. As of January 2021, Lishman was Arsenal's seventh-leading all-time scorer.

8. Eighth on the all-time scoring list for the Gunners is former Dutch international striker and team captain Robin van Persie with 132 markers in 278 matches. He joined the team from Feyenoord in his homeland in the summer of 2004 and helped them win the 2004 Community Shield and 2005 FA Cup. He also won the Premier League's Golden Boot award in 2011-12 with 30 goals in 38 games. Van Persie took home the PFA Players' Player of the Year, the PFA Fans' Player of the Year, the FWA Footballer of the Year, and the Arsenal player of the Season awards that campaign and was named to the PFA Premier League Team of the Year. He promptly disappointed Gunners' fans by engineering a transfer to Manchester United a few months later.

9. Winger Joe Hulme played with the Gunners from 1926 to 1938 after joining from the Blackburn Rovers. The English international racked up 125 goals in 374 games to rank ninth all-time in club scoring and he also helped his squad capture three league titles and a pair of FA Cups. He wasn't eligible for a league winner's medal in 1933-34 as he played just eight games, though he did score five goals in them. Hulme also played cricket for Middlesex and became manager of rivals Tottenham Hotspur between 1945 and 1949 after hanging up his boots.

10. Inside forward/midfielder David Jack of England arrived at Arsenal as a 29-year-old from Bolton for a reported £11,000, which would have been an English record at the time. He debuted for the side in 1928 and won the FA Cup in 1930, along with a trio of league titles and Charity Shields. He notched 34 goals in 1930-31 and retired in 1934 with 124 goals in 208 outings with the club to rank 10th in club history on the all-time scoring list. Jack also tallied three times for England in nine matches.

CONCLUSION

There you go! You've come to the end of this trivia book but certainly not the end of Arsenal's ongoing legacy as one of the world's greatest and most famous soccer clubs.

The first 135 years or so are now at your fingertips and we thank you for allowing us to help you take a look back at the amazing history of the Gunners in a lighthearted and entertaining manner. We also hope you have learned something along the way from our quizzes and "Did You Know" sections.

With this trivia book at your disposal, you are now ready to challenge fellow Gooners and other fans to a variety of quiz contests to prove once and for all who is the most knowledgeable Gunners fan.

We've included information on numerous players and managers as well as club records, trophy successes, transfers, etc.

Please feel free to share the information provided with others and to help teach the team's history to the next generation of soccer supporters.

We haven't been able to include every player and manager in the book, so forgive us if your favorite has been left out. However, you should be able to use the book to complement your knowledge of the club and to test fellow fans on Gunners' history.

There are endless stories surrounding this famous team to accompany facts and figures about its most iconic members. Thank you for taking the time to support the club and relive its memories with us.

Printed in Great Britain
by Amazon

87440379R00077